# Blockchain
# in the Boardroom

Jennifer C. Wolfe

ISBN: 1985722070
ISBN-13: 978-1985722071

# CONTENTS

# 1
## BLOCKCHAIN IN LAYMAN'S TERMS & WHY IT MATTERS

You've probably heard of blockchain, bitcoin and cryptocurrency. But do you know the real impact it will have on our future society? Will it become the new money? Is there more to it than just digital currency? Should your company be investing resources for research and development in it? If so, how much and on what? Who is already way out ahead of the curve and has an extensive patent portfolio on the technology? Could it just be a fad that will soon fade away?

In *Blockchain in the Boardroom*, I summarize the hype about blockchain in layman's terms, why it matters and what you need to know in the boardroom about how it will affect business throughout various industries.

If you are a technologist already familiar with blockchain, you will find this to be an oversimplification; if you continue reading, I apologize to you in advance. If you are a director or C-suite executive trying to get a grasp on the complexities of blockchain and what you really need to know, read on. This is written for you.

Let me start by saying that everything out there about blockchain is incredibly confusing. There are a number of reasons for that confusion. The first is the distraction of bitcoin, which I'll address briefly. The second is that most of the articles and presentations try to explain how blockchain works. The truth is, you don't need to understand how it works.

Just like you don't need to understand how HTML code works to use a website, you won't need to fully understand how blockchain works to make smart business decisions about it. You don't have to understand how the domain name system and internet work to use them. You don't need to understand how all of the processors make your phone work or how apps differ from a regular website. You don't need to know the technical details in the boardroom. You do need to understand what blockchain is, what it can and can't do, what its potential implications for your business are, how long it will take to transform or disrupt your business, and how you compare to others in your industry.

## The Bitcoin Distraction

The most widely publicized use of blockchain right now remains bitcoin and the other 60+ lesser-known forms of cryptocurrency or digital currency (i.e., Litecoin, Zcash, Dash, Ripple, and the list goes on and on). Leading publications like the *Harvard Business Review*, *Economist*, *New York Times*, *Wall Street Journal* and others tend to focus on the surging interest and speculation in these new forms of digital currency and the impact it could have on banking and global currency because it's a hot topic and keeps people coming back, which drives traffic to their publications.

There are already 150 trademarks filed in the U.S. Patent and Trademark Office using some form of the term *bitcoin*. A handful have actually been registered as trademarks including American Bitcoin Exchange and Chicago Bitcoin Exchange (both to a company named Environmental Financial Products). The remaining filings are pending and range from the term itself to words like Bitcoinare, Bitcoin Pizza, Bitcoin Car, Bitcoin Economist and so on. The

Winkelvosses (famous for their role in Facebook and for being early investors in bitcoin) filed a trademark for *Winkelvoss Blended Bitcoin Index* and have already filed a few patents, but most of the other applications have been filed by individuals, most without using an attorney.

When I first heard of bitcoin and blockchain, they sounded like the kind of currency you get in a video game. For me, that currency is worthless because I don't play video games — but for my fifteen-year-old, it's very real because it can buy things he values in those games. That can make it easy for all of us who don't live in those "video game" or "digital" worlds to simply dismiss bitcoin and other cryptocurrencies as "not real."

Jamie Dimon, CEO of JP Morgan, said in October of 2017, "if you're stupid enough to buy bitcoin, you'll pay the price one day," and famously threatened that if he caught his traders trading it, they would be fired. By January of 2018, however, he had changed his mind, stating he regretted calling it a "fraud" and that the blockchain and the potential is real, but bitcoin is still not anything he's interested in. In fact, JP Morgan now has a dedicated initiative they refer to as a "Blockchain Center of Excellence" and has invested in financial tech firms developing blockchain-based solutions. That may leave you wondering what the difference is between blockchain and bitcoin or any of the other cryptocurrencies and the now much-talked-about initial coin offerings. Why is blockchain potentially valuable, but bitcoin is not? I started my search like we all do.

If you go into your Google Browser (or any search engine of choice) and search for "blockchain," you'll be bombarded with ads and sponsored sites of companies either selling consulting or selling bitcoin or other forms of cryptocurrency, or selling software and solutions built on blockchain, many that look like legitimate companies but others that appear questionable. In fact, there is an early adopter company that secured the name "Blockchain" and the domain name www.blockchain.com. This is a company that builds software using blockchain and offers a way to buy and sell digital currency. At first, I thought maybe they invented blockchain, but then I realized that's not the case; they were just first to jump on it as a name.

General internet searches essentially leave you questioning what's credible and what's not, often by writing in a tone that is overly technical or trying to sell you on the services of the company that put the information out there. I moved on to books and attending conferences and interviewing people who claimed to be experts. I pulled videos of experts from IBM and other big companies to listen to them talk about blockchain. Then I re-read the articles and the books, and it finally started to piece together.

What really helped me understand the market potential was doing an in-depth analysis of the patents now of public record that contain the term "blockchain." This is where who was investing in what and why became clear. This, of course, changes weekly, but the analysis at this point in time in the blockchain lifecycle is very telling. It's taken me hours and hours over weeks and months to piece this all together.

What I've done in this short book, *Blockchain in the Boardroom*, is summarize my research down to the basics. What it is, why it matters, how it could be used and what you need to know as you hear and read more about it and confront it in your business.

One caveat: Blockchain is evolving quickly and the technology is in a growth phase with a lot of bugs to work out. A lot of people are writing a lot of things about it, all coming from different points of view and with different agendas. Some are literally "mining" for the gold in the new cryptocurrency coins, while others are building technology solutions that will have lasting impact. The technology is clearly in its early days, so many things will change in the next few years as we all learn more and established companies begin to roll out more concrete use cases.

Based upon my research, blockchain will become a building block to our future, much like other new software and tools have become standards in development, but it has some pitfalls and some big challenges to overcome.

Other than my time in researching and writing this and developing a methodology to analyze the opportunity, I don't have any money invested in blockchain technology solutions or cryptocurrency. I'm not selling software using blockchain or trying to hype some agenda. I present all sides here — the good and the bad. I round out the book with a checklist of questions you should ask of your leadership team and things to consider as you evaluate the impact of blockchain on your business.

## Blockchain in Layman's Terms

In its simplest and crudest form, a blockchain is an advanced form of a database or ledger with verified identities and conditions for what's on each ledger line. As each entry is formed, it creates a "contract" or set of rules governing the information coded in the ledger between the party maintaining the ledger and the individual or property owner on the ledger line. Each entry is an account for something of value (i.e., money, property rights, commodity, etc.). These blocks of ledgers are then strung together using software code (referred to as a hash) that ensures the block can't be altered without both parties agreeing to alter it in a later block. Some people might think of a block as a spreadsheet or a database that is authenticated immediately.

There are some caveats about how it operates, and I'll get into that, but for now, when you hear about something built on blockchain, think of it like any other kind of ledger or database you already know, but with the parties agreeing to its authenticity and information upon creating the line in the ledger.

To understand the concept of blockchain, it helps to go really old school.

Before there was the information technology revolution and centralized databases took over the way we track our accounts, our money, our property records or anything of value, there were handwritten ledgers maintained by people with authority. It might have been a bank or a retailer if you had an account with them. It could have been a local county government that maintained the records by hand of who owned what parcels of property or what automobiles. Even stock transactions were originally maintained in an actual ledger by the corporate secretary. You stood there and watched a person with some authority enter your information into the ledger, thereby creating an understanding between you and the other party of what was in the ledger and what it meant. Blockchain is the same concept: It's a ledger of who has what authenticated by the parties. That's the first part of blockchain — authenticated by the parties, encoded with information and only changeable if both parties agree to a change.

The need for ledgers evolved, of course, as technology advanced and IBM transformed our lives by creating the original SQL-based database (structured query language). Over the years, the complexity of databases grew, as did the ability to centralize and connect databases, ultimately via the internet, but the concept of maintaining a ledger to track your "account" never changed — *how* it was maintained changed dramatically. We've spent the technology revolution advancing and centralizing how we manage accounts so they can be accessed quickly from anywhere via the internet. This has created some problems, which blockchain could solve.

Knowing that blockchain is a type of ledger, I found it helped me to just start thinking of it as a database. I realize that die-hard blockchain technologists will argue that a blockchain can be a database or enhance a database, but not all blockchains are databases. That can be true, and blockchain can do a lot more than just be a database, but if you're trying to get a grasp of this complicated concept, using language and an analogy you already understand can help you bridge the gap to a deeper understanding of how blockchain works and its potential.

Every time you hear someone talk about the blockchain or using blockchain, just think of it as a highly advanced database or ledger of a transaction. It's a way of tracking ownership that is a little different from how we do it today. After you read "blockchain," say the word "database" and see if that starts to help you formulate your thinking about it.

If you begin to grasp the concept of blockchain as a type of underlying technology to a database or ledger or spreadsheet, then you can recognize that we are in a time period similar to the time when IBM, initially, and then companies like Microsoft and Oracle began to transform our world with software connected to databases that had enormous computing power. Just like SQL was the underlying standard for those databases, blockchain could be the underlying standard or conceptual way of managing information and identities in a more secure, efficient and authenticated way than the existing relational databases of today.

Not surprisingly, IBM remains at the forefront of blockchain technology, along with companies like Master Card, Visa, Cisco, Dell, Intel and Wal-Mart (I've analyzed their patent portfolios, along with all patents filed that are now public record related to blockchain, and provide more details later in this book). This is an important indicator because it helps us understand which companies have already invested in the technology, what they are doing with it, what they see as the market potential and how they are carving out their own monopolies on this burgeoning technology. The long-term value opportunities probably are not in unregulated currency, but how it could transform and eliminate inefficiencies and errors in transaction business in the future. The analysis of patents filed is actually one of the most credible and helpful sources of information, because it breaks down how this market is starting to shape up and where your company might fit in it.

To summarize, when you hear the word *blockchain*, think of it as a type of database or ledger. Then think about it like SQL and how companies like Microsoft, IBM and Oracle built software and systems that allowed companies to leverage the power of those databases.

The next question on your mind is likely to be: Why is this different from what we have today or needed?

**Blockchain solves problems in current use of databases and transactions.**

While some say blockchain is a solution looking for a problem, advocates purport that a number of components make blockchain more secure and efficient than the traditional database and how transactions are completed today. But let's start with the problems it is attempting to solve.

I'd like to create a couple of examples to reference. First, consider when you buy a car. You are given temporary license plates from the dealership and then the registration information is submitted to your local government (usually a state bureau of motor vehicles); paper is processed and entered into a database; and then — usually days to weeks later — you receive the registration for your car. An immediate problem you can see is the amount of time it takes to process that transaction. What if it was all done simultaneously at the dealership when you buy the car so your car is registered on a blockchain and no additional work is needed to complete the registration process? This reduces time and transaction costs, possibilities for error and corruption, and improves trust in the process.

Now, let's use a second example. You have an account with a retailer to buy things. They give you a credit card with your account number and you assign a personal identification number (PIN) to use the credit card. Every time you buy something online or in the store, you use the card number and your secret PIN to access your account and buy things of value to you. Now, a hacker comes along and decides to target that retailer and get all of the accounts, user names and PINs. They steal the credit cards in one big bulk cyber attack from millions of customers. (Think Equifax, Target, Yahoo, Uber, etc.)

If that information could be protected and stored in a way that it could not be hacked as easily and made it more difficult to get each account number, PIN, etc., that could solve a lot of problems in an era of cybersecurity war. IBM defines this as solving the fundamental problems of time and trust because blockchain:

1. Saves time on the transaction since it is authenticated the moment the information is entered into the blockchain or database *[car example]*.

2. Removes costs because fewer middlemen are needed to "clear" or authenticate data sets or take steps in the process of entering information in the database and processing it *[car example]*.

3. Reduces risk of tampering, cybersecurity attacks or fraud by decentralizing the way the information is stored *[credit card example]*.

4. Increases trust through shared recordkeeping *[both examples]*.

All of this is done through the underlying code (the way blockchain operates) and processing of the blockchain in what's referred to as a decentralized system — meaning not all in one place for hackers to attack. Three core functions of blockchain allow it to solve some of the problems that plague today's systems:

1. **Decentralized**. This means that the database is in a lot of places at one time and there is no "mother lode" to hack. It doesn't mean it can't be hacked, but it makes it more difficult to hack, thus potentially solving the problem or at least creating more layers of protection in cybersecurity risk management.

2. **Authenticated & Can't Be Changed**. One of the benefits (and also potential downsides) of blockchain is that once it is created, it can't be changed without both parties agreeing to change it or create a new block of information. This addresses a lot of existing concerns about potential corruption or errors and, in theory, creates greater transparency and trust. It also speeds up the process and reduces transaction costs, which, in theory, ultimately benefits both parties.

3. **Smart Contract Capability.** The ability to embed a smart contract into the ledger line is what could reduce significant transaction costs and eliminate steps in the process. This technology has existed for some time, but using it in traditional processes hasn't necessarily made sense. Creating new products and services with blockchain technology as the form of database allows these new smart contracts to reduce time, cost and aggravation in tandem with the other benefits.

Some of the more-technical components of these three big benefits include how cryptography creates public and private keys to store and unlock the data in each ledger line, as well as how hashes are used to connect the blocks of data in a way that can't be altered. In addition, each ledger line is embedded with algorithms or code to create the smart contract capability. Finally, the fact that these blocks are stored on a lot of computers at once, rather than on one centralized computer, collectively solves a number of problems we encounter today.

Essentially, all of the problems we created by building these massive, powerful centralized databases connected through the internet and now to all of our devices can be unraveled by deploying blockchain technology (again, in theory). In the interest of keeping this focused on the business issues, I won't go into more technical detail, but there are technical components to how the major benefits and components of blockchain work. There's *a lot* going on underneath that basic concept, but this is the starting point in conceptually grasping the potential. If it's still confusing, just think of it as an advanced database that can solve some of the problems noted above — and probably some things we don't even realize are a problem yet!

Blockchain is an underlying technology to create more-secure transactions and store encrypted records of ownership. Ownership concepts can range from currency to property, bank accounts, copyrights, trademarks, health records, tracking materials through a supply chain or even, potentially, a universal account — anything you register to own or a secure account you need to establish can be maintained in a blockchain. It has the potential to disrupt every industry and every profession that manages these societal functions right now: banks, governments, credit card companies, insurance companies, rights management companies (i.e., music, photos, video), lawyers, accountants, architects, musicians, producers, healthcare record management, doctors, hospitals and so on.

There's still a lot to be done for blockchain to become mainstream, and I cover more of that in Chapter Four, but that work is already underway and you should be thinking about blockchain as a future underlying technology for how transactions are processed and stored.

### Blockchain & the Domain Name System

If you are struggling with the concept of decentralization or the distributed ledger component of blockchain, don't worry — you are not alone. This is one of the more difficult concepts to grasp. The most relatable example of a distributed database functioning today is the domain name system. You may not fully understand the underlying technology of how your web browser goes out to the internet and finds a website you want to see so it appears before you on your computer or device, but it is operating as a distributed database of names and numbers.

For the world to be connected via the internet requires the domain name system, with a set of standards and rules created by the Internet Corporation for Assigned Names & Numbers (ICANN). This organization sets the governing principles by which the registries (like Verisign running Dot Com) and registrars like a GoDaddy where you register names (i.e., Google.com) operate. It is these companies that connect the world through a distributed name server network. Just because one server goes down does not mean everything goes down. The information is distributed out among many computer servers and connected through the global domain name system.

Every domain name or internet address you use is actually a string of numbers behind the names. The concept of a public/private key string (the cryptography) of numbers in the blockchain is not that different from the string of numbers you know as a domain name like Amazon.com. In Chapter Three, I provide more detail about how we might historically consider the way the internet formed and is now connected to how blockchain might function in the future as a building block to transactions. For now, recognize that we currently have a global distributed ledger concept well at work for all of us — the World Wide Web.

## Skepticism Remains in the Headlines

Even with all the promises of greater security, validity and efficiency, if you remain initially skeptical of blockchain, it's with good reason. With all the problems it purports to solve, we are seeing one headline after another of the currency blockchains being hacked. Does that mean blockchain doesn't really work?

Take a look at these headlines:

- "How Bitcoin is Stolen; 5 Common Threats," *Fortune* magazine
- "More than $70 million stolen in bitcoin hack," CNN Money
- "Bitcoin: $64 million in cryptocurrency stolen in sophisticated hack, exchange says," *The Guardian*
- "Bitcoin Worth Millions Stolen Days Before US Exchange Opens," *US News*

This is just a handful of headlines from major news outlets in— and there have been countless more, week and after week since then. What is all the hype about if blockchain — or bitcoins — can be hacked like anything else? I thought one of the advantages of blockchain was that it was hackproof. The truth is, it could be safer than anything else out there, but a lot will need to be done to make it that way.

*[See sidebar next page]*

I'll sidebar here for just a minute on bitcoin because that's what is in the headlines right now. If you acquire bitcoin and want to convert it to U.S. dollars (or other government backed currency), you have to go through an exchange. This is a business that trades or exchanges bitcoins. It is currently not regulated like banks are regulated. Those exchanges then hold onto your bitcoin while they transact business for you and take a fee and ultimately allow you to either just trade it for other digital currency or cash out for actual dollars or other foreign currency. Those "hacks" you read about in the headlines occurred on the exchanges while they were holding bitcoin.

In most cases, the hacks occur because a bad guy wants to steal bitcoin, which can't be tracked, and the exchanges use a two-factor authentication process to grant access to you, the account holder, to the block and to reset a password. These hacks occur much like any other. Hackers track what you are doing (i.e., investing in bitcoin) on social media (because you put everything out there); they hijack your mobile phone number (which is easy to attain because you plaster it all over everything and/or is sold by your provider); reset the login to the exchange (which functions like all other login-password websites); and then unlock your account, get access to your account and take your bitcoin. Because bitcoin is currently unregulated and not tracked the same way bank accounts are, there's little recourse.

This is one of the reasons many exchanges are now eliminating anonymity of users and stepping up multi-factor authentication for account users.

As you can see, it's the exchanges using traditional hackable technology for authentication that were hacked, not the blockchain itself. An important point in this is that blockchain is only more secure *if* you protect the identity of your private key. However, the reality is that in many exchanges, the consumer doesn't even have the key (they are using traditional login technology); but rather the exchange maintains the public and private key and manages access to the blockchain on behalf of the customer – much like a traditional bank. Meaning, we are back to the same problems – this is one of the big challenges in cryptocurrency. An exchange (i.e. bank) is still needed and they are still using traditional centralized hackable technology that can be compromised – so where does that leave us?

Another area that causes concern for a lot of mainstream business is the initial rationale behind bitcoin and cryptocurrency. Many believe that governments and businesses can't be trusted and they don't want everything they do being tracked or regulated by government authorities. They might be concerned about inaccuracies in the process or potential for corruption, or simply want a form of currency they can use anywhere in the world that is not subject to manipulation by central authorities. For example, today, your property is registered with the government, your banking is registered with your government-issued Social Security Number, you must pay taxes on income tracked by the government, etc. Many do not like this and are looking for forms of trading things of value (i.e., currency or property) with anonymity in a way that can't be tracked. This motivation for the rapid growth of bitcoin and other crypto currencies is what gives rise to alarm from government and traditional financial institutions.

Despite these initial concerns, there are some real opportunities to explore in how the blockchain concept and technology could work. Let's look outside of cryptocurrency. At a macro level, some of the big potential disruptions that could occur are mapped out on the chart on the next page — a quick snapshot of the industries and functions to be affected. *[See chart next page]*

## Financial Services

- Letters of credit
- Cross-currency payments
- Mortgages
- Processing transactions

## Government

- Land registry and ownership
- Vehicle registry and ownership
- Citizen identification

## Healthcare

- Medical records
- Pharmaceutical supply & tracking

## Insurance

- Claims processing
- Internet of Things integration for policy monitoring

## Manufacturing

- Supply chain tracking
- Products, parts & logistics tracking
- Maintenance records
- Internet of Things

## Food Supply

- From farm to table

## Media

- Digital rights in music, movies, photographs, trademarks and intellectual property

The potential for blockchain as a new standard in smart contracts and database management is far reaching. In the next chapter, I detail what's happening out there in blockchain outside of the cryptocurrency fad. But before we move on, consider a few takeaway points for understanding blockchain:

- A transaction on a blockchain ledger could represent anything:

  - A credit account that allows you to buy things with it and replenish that credit

  - A piece of property you might sell

  - Digital rights to a song, photograph, video, etc., that you want to monetize

  - Access to a secure box that has a piece of jewelry you want to sell

  - An insurance policy

  - Information about your health

  - The whereabouts of a product in a supply chain or manufacturing process

  - Your very identity as a whole — everything about you, and the ability to transact whatever business you need in a secure manner

  - The potential to be used to track anything of value.

- Every time you hear the word blockchain, add the word database or think of an old school ledger, and it will all start to make a lot more sense.

- Blockchain is attempting to solve the existing exposure to cyber attacks on credit cards, Social Security Numbers and other identifiable information in three ways:

o Using cryptography (a string of numbers) required to access your "account" or line in a ledger in a block of ledgers; has the technology to ensure that can't be changed without your authority.

o Embedding smart contract codes into the ledger line to eliminate steps and processes based upon the outcome of certain transaction-based events.

o Storing the ledger on multiple computer systems (distributed or decentralized) at the same time that are updated concurrently using software and network capabilities being developed by companies like IBM, Microsoft, Oracle, etc., and verified by the participants in the block. This will allow it to be harder to be attacked because it exists in more than one place at one time.

- Today, you can't just go online and access a blockchain. It requires special software that has not yet become mainstream.

- In this model, no single system controls the blockchain.

- **_Brief Comment on Bitcoin_**: Bitcoin currency is stored and built in a blockchain ledger. It was created as a way to trade currency anonymously. You may have heard people talk about "mining" bitcoin. This is unique to bitcoin currency and not necessarily a component to all uses of blockchain. When bitcoin was first released, to obtain a bitcoin, you had to digitally "mine" for it by solving complex math problems. The bitcoin blockchain was created to have a finite number of bitcoins available (21 million).

o If you "mine" the bitcoin, you get the coin or "currency" in the bitcoin world. As more bitcoin were mined or obtained by solving a math problem, the math problems got harder and harder. Today, only approximately 4 million bitcoins remain to be mined. At a value of approximately US$9,300 per bitcoin (at the time of this writing), that means there is approximately $37 million available in bitcoin to still mine. To do so requires so much computing power that rooms full of computer servers are needed to solve it. In fact, it's creating power shortages in China because it takes so much server power to solve the increasingly difficult math problems.

o The fact that there is a finite amount of bitcoin is why the value keeps going up. Once it is all mined, then all you can do is trade it or exchange it. This is why many see it as a Ponzi scheme. What happens when no one values the bitcoin and no one will trade it for anything of value? That's the potential problem with bitcoin, or any of these digital currencies: It's only valuable as long as the people trading it are willing to give you something of value. Just keep in mind that bitcoin was created using blockchain as the underlying technology, but not all blockchain uses have to be for unregulated currency.

- The American National Standards Institute (ANSI; a nonprofit organization) governs the standards that governments and businesses use to develop systems like SQL as relational database management systems. It sets the standards by which databases, information services and software are developed to create consistencies in operations that operate across governments and organizations so it benefits everyone. We have relied upon this as a society for decades, most of us completely unaware of it. Some similar form of standards in blockchain will be needed in the future. There are already organizations out there trying to do this.

- The Internet Corporation for Assigned Names & Numbers (ICANN) sets policy that governs how the internet connects through a distributed set of name servers. The same type of global policy or governing body may be needed.

- Blockchain does not yet have standards. It will need standards and consistency for companies to leverage it — but those very standards can also open the door to the same problems we have today. (More on this in Chapter Four.)

- Blockchain is not a relational or connected database. It's maintained separately and connected by many computers.

- An important indicator that directors and executives need to understand the impact of this on their business now is that nearly 500 patents related to blockchain technology already have been publicly posted in the USPTO. The companies that figure this out and protect it properly will have a clear competitive edge. Those that wait may find themselves boxed out or paying hefty licensing fees to use the new blockchain technology.

## DECENTRALIZATION MAY BE THE FUTURE

In the latter half of the 20th century, centralization became the key to databases amassing enormous power and potential and creating enormous economies of scale. In the second half of this century, we are likely to see decentralization as the emergent form of connectivity to address the problems that have emerged in cybersecurity. We made a lot of really big targets. Now we have to unravel that.

# 2
## MARKETPLACE INDICATORS

With a basic understanding of blockchain as an advanced database and transaction technology, let's take a look at what's happening in today's marketplace and what that can forecast about the future. Several sources of information provide important indicators.

1.  **Established companies rolling out blockchain-related technology**. These large financial, technology, retail and consulting companies are building out products and solutions using blockchain. They often publicly post videos of presentations, slide decks and detailed research briefings that are available and typically well-written and solid in the research. While their information is underpinned by the agenda of selling their products, they put out some of the best and most comprehensive explanations of the problems that blockchain solves and actual use cases being developed.

2.  **Start-up and emerging companies paving new roads and launching new ideas**. Wherever there is a charismatic CEO-type leader and access to big venture capital in a hot new area, there will undoubtedly be thousands of start-ups all over the world. Most will fail. However, a few will be nimble and agile enough to survive and find the future. While there are far too

many start-ups in blockchain to highlight even a fraction of them in this book, a focused search can look for the top and fastest-growing ones to ascertain what is developing. I've pulled a few of the ones that have enough money invested to ride the potential years ahead of losing money before the breakthrough.

3. **Patents & trademarks filed in the USPTO**. This is the most-credible source of information because it is public and transparent, and written to meet the standards of a patent — new, novel and non-obvious. Patents provide a description of the invention in detail, along with the background of why it is important. This is probably the most-important analysis because it gives a true picture of what companies are developing that they believe is worth protecting. It's also quite cumbersome to do the research, but the most rewarding in the payoff. A cursory search of trademarks can also provide key signals for the types of marketing and branding campaigns that companies are exploring to roll out.

4. **Media coverage.** This is the final and, honestly, least-credible source of information. Media today is so 24–7 focused that most (not all) pieces are laced with inaccuracies, or failure to confirm or check facts due to time constraints. They are also responding to what's the news of the day to keep people coming back with provocative — and sometimes misleading — information. Obviously, some publications carry more weight than bloggers out there with an agenda. However, stacking up headlines over time and looking for trends in media coverage is very telling in how the space is developing and looking historically at when a new area shifts from being a hot trending topic to being a substantive technology that will begin to transform.

This chapter breaks down the marketplace indicators into these key categories. Before providing a company by company summary, it's helpful to understand that there are two prominent "projects" or platforms currently being developed and used by companies today: Ethereum and IBM's Linux Hyperledger. The tables that follow summarize what the blockchain project is and the companies partnering or collaborating to build standards and technologies using their platforms.

You will see some overlap. Both of these organizations are functioning as nonprofits, with a goal of developing an open source product to leverage, scale and develop standards and to further blockchain initiatives across companies and industries.

An important note is that the Ethereum Network Alliance is separate from the Ethereum Platform and Ether Currency. The public Ethereum project allows users and developers to create their own tokens or currency. The Alliance is a group of companies working to build open source standardization using the Ethereum Platform. Ether is a currency that fuels the platform, but is not necessarily required to be part of the Alliance. Likewise, IBM is a leader in the Linux Foundation's Hyperledger Project, but it also has its own blockchain initiatives, many of which could be patented as described later in this chapter.

Another important distinction as we address these two big platforms versus what individual companies are doing is that these projects are open source, meaning they do not claim proprietary rights to the code/platform being developed. When I detail many of the companies that have filed patents, those patents are distinctive from the open source platform they may use as an underlying technology.

Another important component is understanding which blockchain networks are private versus public. Blockchain can be used in a way that is private or semi-private, or it can be developed to be completely open, transparent and public. Most commercial use will ultimately be private or semi-private. Hyperledger is a permissioned and private network, whereas Ethereum can be public, private or semi-private.

## Ethereum Alliance

- **What It Is**
  - A blockchain-based platform to run smart contracts.
  - For developers to create markets, store registries of debts, move funds or other transactions without middlemen.
  - Open Source Standardization — not a product.
  - Evolving in tandem with a separate public Ethereum blockchain (cryptocurrency) network.
  - Nonprofit organization.
- **Prominent Companies Using It**
  - Accenture
  - Broadridge
  - BNY Mellon
  - Credit Suisse
  - Cognizant
  - Deloitte
  - JP Morgan
  - Intel
  - ING
  - Infosys
  - Microsoft
  - National Bank of Canada
  - Pfizer
  - Samsung
  - Toyota Research
  - UBS

## Hyperledger

- **What It Is**
  - An open source collaborative effort to advance blockchain technologies across industries; a global collaboration hosted by the Linux Foundation (a nonprofit).
- **Prominent Companies Using It**
  - Accenture
  - Airbus
  - American Express
  - Baidu
  - Cisco
  - Deloitte
  - Digital Asset
  - EY
  - Fujitsu
  - GM Financial
  - Hitachi
  - IBM
  - Intel
  - JP Morgan
  - Lilly
  - Oracle
  - PWC
  - SAP
  - Samsung

## Established Companies

Several established companies come to the forefront in developing new products, technologies and solutions using blockchain. There's a lot of detail in what they are doing, so I've included only highlights here.

*IBM* was early in to develop a global community of blockchain developers through its Linux Hypderledger project. It is quickly developing a governing board and principles to guide it, creating greater legitimacy and credibility to the burgeoning technology and to shield it from the criticism of cryptocurrencies. Some of their premiere project partners are listed in the table on the previous page.

The project is an open source collaborative effort to advance cross-industry blockchain technologies. The Linux Foundation is the host of the Hyperledger project. One of the key distinctions of the IBM Hyperledger project is that it is not for cryptocurrency. Its purpose is to leverage the broader business possibilities of creating confidential transactions in a distributed network that is programmable with the embedded logic of smart contracts.

Many companies will continue to partner up with IBM in understanding, investigating and using blockchain technology. An important component of this partnership is that you are "marrying yourself" to the blockchain platform and technology that IBM is building, so, if you are exploring a blockchain research and development process, give yourself some checkpoints to evaluate if other technology solutions are developing that you also want to experiment with in your development plan. To access IBM's hyperledger requires a specific API for interacting with their peer nodes (i.e., computers). This is because the hyperledger blockchain is truly its own internet environment and you need those tools to access it. You can't use a traditional web browser to access it. This inherently means those involved are a bit more tech-savvy than average.

In the patent analysis below, I detail more about their patent portfolio. IBM has the legacy of rolling out new technologies that transform society from their rise through the 1960s and 1970s as the predominant database and computing company. Will they do the same here? They have certainly positioned themselves to be a leader in developing the governing principles and standards, and undoubtedly have scores of people working on the technology, the solutions and how to monetize it.

**AXA Insurance** has rolled out a simple and easy-to-understand, consumer-based product using blockchain (on Ethereum's platform). Known as Fizzy, it has a travel insurance program that is built using blockchain technology. They currently provide travel insurance for transcontinental flights between the U.S. and France. That's a pretty narrow product service, but a great example of how narrow and niched these products can be.

Here's how it works.

Go to their website: www.fizzy.axa (I explain how their top-level domain AXA works and why that's important in the next chapter).

Enter your flight number and agree upon a price to pay for insurance if that flight is more than two hours late. The Fizzy algorithm determines the price for that flight and the payout if it is late. If you agree, you enter into a transaction with them. You interface with their website like you would any other transaction, but the underlying technology is using blockchain and Ethereum. When you pay the price, it forms a smart contract encoded with the algorithm necessary to determine whether your flight is more than two hours late and the contract is stored in a ledger line in a block chain. As each transaction is recorded by new customers, the block continues to build and can't be changed — once you buy it, you bought it; you can't change your mind when you see the weather report for clear skies that day.

The day of your flight comes. If your flight is on time, then AXA keeps your money; end of transaction. If your flight is more than two hours late, the encoded algorithm recognizes this and automatically pays you the requisite insurance proceeds, and the transaction is complete.

This is a great and easy example of how blockchain works to make transactions seamless. You, as the consumer, don't even know it's being done on the blockchain, but for AXA, it is creating more efficiencies, fewer places where human error can occur and an automated process.

Now, certainly, problems can and probably will arise, but this is a nice example of how it can play out. "The use of the smart contract to trigger claims will add trust in the insurer and policyholder relationship," said AXA representative Jean-Bapitse Mounteir in a conversation with CoinDesk. Payouts under Fizzy are made to the customer using government-issued currencies rather than cryptocurrency.

Another important point here is how the Ethereum Network works. They have created their own alternative root zone of the internet known as .ETH. Their blockchain is built using .ETH. The AXA product has used a domain name that can be accessed by consumers on any web browser, but the underlying technology is running in the background on a different system.

**Intel** is a member of the Enterprise Ethereum Alliance and Hyperledger (by IBM; described above ). It is also a partner of the Initiative for Cryptocurrencies & Contracts, an academic group researching how blockchain solutions may affect the financial industry. Intel named its distributed ledger platform SawtoothLake, and then contributed it to the Hyperledger project as open source to advance the growth of blockchain. Intel is also working with the R3 Consortium and academic bodies such as the Initiative for CryptoCurrencies & Contracts.

A company like Intel has to understand how the technology can produce microprocessors to leverage the blockchain advantages and overcome the challenges presented. It has already positioned itself as a leader not just in developing the core technology that will be needed, but in leading the way for standardization.

**Microsoft** is also investing in blockchain research, particularly related to the cloud platform and how blockchain may transform offerings in the cloud. In that regard, blockchain as a service could become an offering by Microsoft. Already benefiting from the millions of businesses working with Microsoft products, servers and cloud-based offerings, Microsoft adding a blockchain component would leverage that marketplace potentially faster than newcomers. Microsoft is a founding member of the Enterprise Ethereum Alliance.

**SAP** began to get publicly involved in blockchain in 2016 with a bottom-up approach in its innovation labs. By mid-year, it had collaborated with blockchain start-up Ripple on a cross-border payment proof of concept to transmit funds between Canada and Germany. SAP is also investigating cloud-delivered integrated offerings.

**Wal-Mart** is out in the forefront and not necessarily in the way you might imagine. They have partnered with IBM's hyper-ledger project and have built a Food Safety Alliance. They have also partnered with 10 food suppliers to improve how produce is tracked from farm to store to better manage inventory and food safety for its customers using blockchain technology.

Their food supplier partners include Dole, Driscoll's Golden State Foods, Kroger, McCormick and Company, McLane Company, Nestle, Tyson Foods, and Unilever. By applying blockchain to trace food in the distribution process, they were able to cut the time it took to trace a package of mangoes from the farm to the store to just 2 seconds — from days or weeks. They are working to create a standards-based method of collecting data about the origin, safety and authenticity of food using blockchain for traceability throughout the supply chain.

Not surprisingly, Wal-Mart also is filing patents using blockchain, but not related to food safety (see below). These organizations are now working to build standards for collecting data about the origin, safety and authenticity of food using this technology. The vision of the pilot program is to encourage accountability and provide suppliers, regulators and consumers with greater insight and transparency into how food is handled from the farm to the fork.

The **Bank of New York Mellon** is using blockchain to accelerate and design the development of unique applications for securities lending, using blockchain to trade and transfer assets.

**Mizuho Financial** is using blockchain for settlements using virtual currency.

**Credit Mutuel Arkea** is using blockchain to manage customer identity and improve customer satisfaction.

**Pfizer** is partnering with the Ethereum Alliance to develop systems designed to keep counterfeit goods out of medical supply chains. This MediLedger project is slated to go through various tests via a partnership with Genentech.

**DTCC**, as an industry-owned and -governed financial market utility, is recognizing the potential of blockchain in the future. It, too, has joined the Enterprise Ethereum Alliance to explore and embrace the disruption that could emerge.

**JP Morgan** has a web page dedicated to blockchain technology (see www.jpmorgan.com/global/blockchain) touting its Blockchain

Center of Excellence in exploring use cases and pilot solutions across business lines. They have formed strategic relationships with key vendors such as Digital Asset Holdings, Axoni, Enterprise Ethereum, Alliance and Hyperledger.

**Amazon Web Services** is investing in blockchain through a partner approach as well. They are currently seeking proposals from companies innovating in healthcare and life sciences, financial services, supply chain management, security, and compliance. Amazon has partnered with Sawtooth (Intel), Corda R3, PokitDok and Samsung Nexledger. It's also working with Wuorum, an Ethereum-based distributed ledger protocol for the financial services industry, as well as companies like BlockApps, Virtusa Polaris, PWC and Deloitte. AWS is also on the cutting edge of potential new currencies, working with Luno and Coinbase.

**Samsung's NexLedger** is a solutions-oriented blockchain product to create digital identities, digital payments, stamping and other services for customers. This is their proprietary blockchain platform, which could also become a foundation for how companies leverage the technology.

**T-Mobile** is developing digital identity and authentication tools using Sawtooth, the Intel Hyperledger project. They are partnering with Amazon Web Services to explore how these services may work in the future.

**Facebook** does not appear to have publicly known blockchain projects. Mark Zuckerberg, Facebook's CEO, announced in his 2018 new year's speech that he plans to study encryption and blockchain "to see how to best use them in our services." He just recently announced an internal team evaluating their options and by the end of the year we are likely see Facebook begin to partner with some of the existing projects or, perhaps, start its own. With their enormous global power of influence over billions of people, they have interesting opportunities and the potential to disrupt industries in a similar vein to Amazon.

**Google** has been one of the more active corporate investors in blockchain activity, according to Bloomberg Technology, ranking second in size of investments with six investments in data storage provider Storj, cryptocurrency derivatives trading platform Ledger X and merchant services with Veem. It's reported that Google's DeepMind artificial intelligence lab is embracing blockchain, potentially specifically looking at healthcare implications. While it, too, does not yet appear to be part of one of the big projects, it is undoubtedly working stealthily behind the scenes and will go public when it's ready. Its patent portfolio is small relative to the cutting-edge work Google is doing in smart home technology and driverless cars, but that probably will change in the future.

Of course, big consulting companies like **Accenture**, **EY**, **PWC**, **Broadridge**, **Cognizant and Deloitte** have all rolled out extensive practices in blockchain and cryptocurrency to provide comprehensive strategies and solutions for companies trying to tackle the new technology. PWC has been working with Guidewire, an insurance platform, to use blockchain-based smart contracts to auto-approve claims and trigger payments, thereby removing the need for manual intervention. It is also built with Amazon Web Services such as AWS Identity and Access Management.

**Disney** built a blockchain, aptly named Dragonchain, which could compete with the Ethereum platform. Dragonchain is designed to be more private than other popular blockchains like bitcoin or Ethereum. Out of its tech-focused Seattle office, the company started building the blockchain protocol in 2014 to create a secure assets-management system for internal use. In 2016, they decided to drop the project and make it open source, allowing several employees to form the Dragon Foundation, a nonprofit that will keep the open source project going. They are currently pursuing fundraising efforts to continue the research they started several years ago, including an initial coin offering.

We see much more of what established companies are doing by studying their patent filings, but this highlights a few of the more widely publicized uses by established institutions.

If one thing should be clear in reading just these short synopses of what big companies are doing, it's that they are already partnering and forming alliances, and standardizing how they will build new products and services. No one company is out on its own trying to tackle this one. The revolution by blockchain will not be done alone. This is all the more reason your company may want to consider getting involved in one of the open source projects or joining some of the efforts already underway.

## Start-up & Emerging Companies

There are probably thousands of start-ups out there right now developing software and tools or new forms of cryptocurrency and exchanges related to blockchain in some way. I've listed a few of the better-known ones that have acquired significant funding and a brief summary of what they are doing.

- **Digital Asset Holdings**. Led by Blythe Masters, the former JP Morgan executive who invented the credit default swap, the company has raised more than $110 million from big banks and investors, including JP Morgan, Broadridge, Goldman Sachs, PNC and others. They are one of the leading financial tech firms in blockchain, developing the software and products that will transform banking and securities. Their products include new ways of managing equities, fixed income, repurchase agreements and platform solutions. With offices scattered around the world, they are poised to be one of the leaders in the way banks and financial institutions implement blockchain solutions.

- **Blockchain.** Blockchain is a blend of a consultant and developer with an exchange for virtual currency. They have raised $70 million from Silicon Valley, Wall Street and London, including Sir Richard Branson and Google Ventures. Led by Peter Smith, the firm is focused on helping businesses begin to accept bitcoin or virtual currency by signing up with its and its their technology.

- **Coinbase.** Backed by Andreessen Horowitz, and other big tech VC funds, they have raised more than $200 million to build one of the most-popular exchanges for bitcoin, Ethereum and Litecoin cryptocurrencies.

- **Circle**. Backed by Goldman Sachs, they have raised more than $136 million. While they began as an exchange of cryptocurrencies with a heavy PR effort in traditional publications like the *Wall Street Journal, Forbes*, the *New York Times* and *Financial Times*, they are moving into mobile payments.

- **21 Inc**. Backed by Cisco Investments and Andreessen Horowitz, they have raised more than $100 million. Starting as a bitcoin-based exchange, they are evolving and expanding into IOT, micropayments and e-mail platforms.

- **Ripple**. Backed by Accenture, Google Ventures and big Silicon Valley venture funds, they have raised close to $100 million as one of the top growing cryptocurrencies focused on global payments.

- **Bitfury**. Backed by big venture capital funds, it has raised close to $90 million and touts itself as a leading full-service blockchain solutions company, including software and hardware offerings.

- **Lisk.** Lisk is dedicated to infrastructure and development of a blockchain network. It raised funds through an Initial Coin Offering and is on the forefront of education and outreach.

- **NameCoin.** This start-up is an open source technology aimed at revolutionizing the domain name system. It has created a digital currency of names and a decentralized manner of protecting free speech rights resistant to censorship. The coins can be used to create keys that are used in other cryptocurrencies, as well as access websites using the alternative root of .Bit.

- **Venture capital firms.** According to a CB Insights report, the most-active venture capital firms investing in blockchain-based companies, based upon portfolio companies from 2012–2017 include:

  o Digital Currency Group

  o Blockchain Capital

  o Pantera Capital

  o Draper Associations

  o 500 Start-ups

  o RRE Ventures

  o Fenbushi Capital

  o Andreessen Horowitz

  o Plug & Play Ventures

  o Liberty City Ventures

There are long lists of cryptocurrency-based start-ups either forming exchanges or developing their own forms of crypto currency — more than we could possibly cover in a macro trend book like this. Among the top blockchain start-up lists for 2018, here are a few other names you may want to know.

  o **Ark**. All-in-one blockchain solution available to users, developers and start-ups, creating an ecosystem in the European union.

  o **Extra Credit**. Proclaiming it as the first education cryptocurrency, the company rewards users in its own cryptocurrency for learning about blockchains and taking tests online.

- o **Trust Token**. Offers users across the world the ability to turn a real world asset into a cryptocurrency token, which allows anyone to create liquid and fractional ownership for an asset.

- o **Thrive**. A community-based system that rewards publishers and consumers all over the world, this claims to be the premium decentralized advertising marketplace.

- o **Cypherium**. A public blockchain system developed by executives from Amazon, Google and Microsoft, they are addressing how to build the infrastructure and governance system needed to solve the problems blockchain will face for scaled commercial viability. They hope to bring cryptocurrencies into the mainstream.

**According to *Fortune*, the top 6 cryptocurrencies are**:

- Ethereum

- Ripple

- Cardano

- NEO

- NEM

- Stellar

I briefly comment on the challenges of cryptocurrencies in Chapter Four, but I encourage you to stay focused on the longer-term implications of blockchain. Cryptocurrencies are not any different from the dot-com bubble of the 1990s. It will burst at some point. I list some references and resources if this is of interest, but in the boardroom, I see the bigger focus as watching the technology and implications for existing business functions.

That said, keep an eye on cryptocurrencies. It's possible one of them could survive the hype and the inevitable fall, and become something you later accept and trade as an asset of value.

- A few other interesting new companies are using blockchain technology.

  o **Cognate** uses blockchain to create permanent, timestamped records of "use" of a trademark. In order to enforce and defend trademark rights, trademark owners must be able to prove where, when, and how their marks are used. Cognate has developed a cutting edge approach to recording proof of use for companies of all sizes.

  o **ShipChain** is a blockchain-based logistics product to help track shipping. This one has larger business applications beyond cryptocurrency and is one to watch.

  o **ConnectJob** is a blockchain-based marketplace for on-demand services that aims to replace companies like Uber, Lift or Taskrabbit.

  o **Experty** is a voice and video calling application similar to Skype or Viber. Experty lets individual experts embed and share their user profiles where they want to market themselves. Users seeking advice from experts will be able to use the application to make a call and use tokens to pay for the time spent.

  o **Oden** is an online education platform based on blockchain to allow students and teachers to interact directly.

  o **Steemit** is a blockchain-based social media company that pays users for submitting content.

## The Blockchain Stock Boost

Another interesting phenomenon is the recent surge in stock prices for companies that announce a blockchain component to their business, or even just change the name. In December 2017, *Bloomberg News* reported that the Long Island Ice Tea Corp.'s shares rose 289 percent after it rebranded itself Long Blockchain Corp. The company had been selling non-alcoholic beverages, but announced it would now seek to partner with or invest in companies that develop blockchain technologies.

In January, it was announced that Kodak, emerging from the shadows of its 2012 bankruptcy, loaned its name to a new digital currency called KodakCoin, which will help photographers manage their digital rights. Kodak's stock rose more than 200 percent following the announcement. KodakCoin will have an initial coin offering. If you are not familiar with an initial coin offering, it's similar to raising money for a start-up company, which requires that investors are qualified investors (i.e., a net worth greater than $1 million and/or annual revenue greater than $200,000). The currency is worth whatever those buying and selling it determine it to be, much like a start-up valuation by venture capitalists or early investors.

Many new cryptocurrencies are forming using blockchain technology and preparing their own "initial coin offerings." Some of these companies will "go public" with such initial coin offerings, where they ostensibly create their own currency offerings. As they create their own "tokens" or currencies, the question of how we pay for things in the future remains at the forefront of how these companies will succeed or fail.

Is this the same irrational exuberance that existed in the 1990s during the dot-com bubble? I don't think we're even there yet. This is just the giddy excitement that comes from something new to talk about and invest in. Money is certainly being dumped, but the irrational exuberance comes when a lot of people start making a lot more money from it. If you recall what happened back then, a lot of money was poured into start-ups claiming themselves to be part of the "new economy" or "dot-com" era. Most of them failed miserably, but a few emerged. We are at that same point with blockchain, except this time, the big players like IBM and Microsoft jumped into the deep end of the pool early.

## Patents & Trademarks

As of early 2018, there are approximately 500 patents in the United States Patent & Trademark Office database that contain the word "blockchain" somewhere in the application. Undoubtedly, there are hundreds more in process right now and that number will rise at an accelerating pace by the end of the year. This gives us a perfect snapshot of where the industry is in early days and it will be helpful historically to look back on this moment in time as we try to make sense of the blockchain age.

While many are the work of individual inventors or unknown start-up companies, a majority are being filed by large, well-known companies. I have summarized the highlights in this chapter. To be clear, many of these are still patents in process. They may or may not ultimately be registered as a patent, but are now public record. This indicates the investment in the technology by the company and an explanation of how they have done it. First, let's start with a general breakdown.

In doing the research for this book, I extracted all of the patents through February 2018 containing the word blockchain. I then categorized these based upon a few general buckets of functionality that will be part of the blockchain use case: data integrity, identification, smart contracts or financial transactions. If there was something unique about the patent or it related to a specific industry, I categorized it accordingly; for example, if it was related to artwork or coupons or biometric technology. Anything that didn't fit easily into one of those categories went into an other category.

I've dropped in a chart of how the patents break down by category on the next page. What a more-detailed analysis shows is that these companies are trying to create proprietary methods to solve some of the bigger problems of blockchain, as well as carve out specific niches that could give them a monopoly or license rights into the future.

It's important to note that patents can take up to 12 month or sometimes more to become public record, so this snapshot is in a bit of a lag, but still helpful. Hyperledger and Ethereum are both open source projects, so they do not patent their development, but rather open it up to accelerate development. Accordingly, these patents are what companies are trying to put a wall around and protect as proprietary technology.

The heaviest areas of investment at these early stages are not entirely surprising, since they relate to building the network or platform, creating identification mechanisms, or securing the integrity of the data. Top areas include financial transactions, land or vehicle registration, media, voting, and biometric and crowdsourcing. A few interesting categories had a handful of patents in those areas, shown in the chart.

*[See chart next page]*

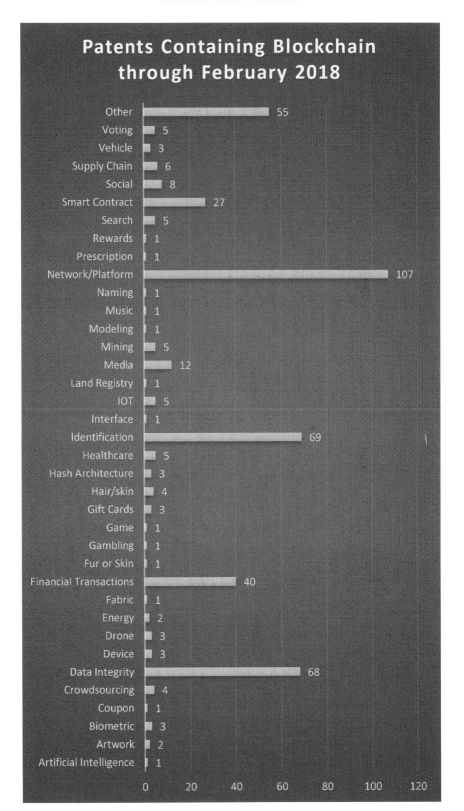

Patents Containing Blockchain through February 2018

As I continue to evaluate monthly new reports, we can see these areas will grow quickly. Now, let's get a snapshot of how the big, well-known companies compare to one another in terms of the size of their portfolio. To make this more meaningful, I focused on large, well-known companies or highly funded start-ups with more than three active patents as of January 2018. At the top of the list is Bank of America, followed by Mastercard, IBM, FMR, Intel and Accenture. Not making the top of list were Microsoft and Oracle.

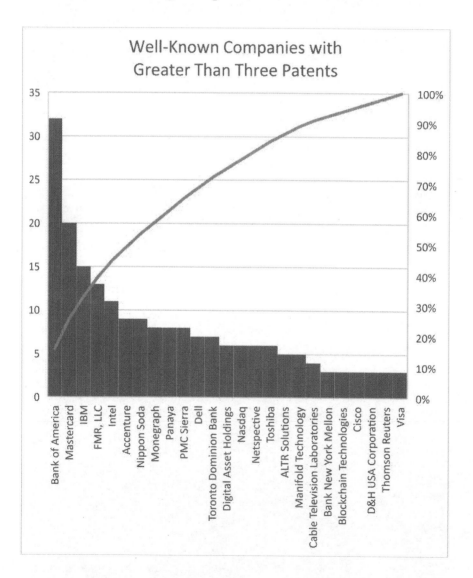

Well-Known Companies with Greater Than Three Patents

I've summarized the broad overview of portfolios (listed alphabetically). (If you're interested in following my patent analytics, subscribe to my blog. I'll be reporting on it regularly.)

## Accenture

The big consulting giant has a developing patent portfolio of rewritable blockchain, creating a trust framework for platform data using blockchain and selecting commodity suppliers through a blockchain-based database.

## Avaya

Avaya has developed a smartphone-fraud proof authorization and authentication for secure transactions using blockchain. The insurance company is undoubtedly considering how to make it easier for consumers to securely transact on the go in the future.

## Bank of America

Bank of America is leading the way with filings by a bank with 32 filings. No other bank comes close to where they are in terms of developing and protecting blockchain technology for themselves. They are clearly looking to protect all corners of what blockchain can do (reduce time and processing, improve identity verification, eliminate hackability). Worth noting is that some companies are jumping in and building their own portfolios, while others are just partnering up with IBM, Ethereum or others. Here is just a sampling of the concepts Bank of America is protecting:

- Security and access in a distributed network
- Large-scale processing using block chain
- Enhancing blockchain-based security with biometrics
- Routing data
- Separate security features

- Validation of instruments
- Self-managing rewards program using blockchain
- Alias for person-to-person payments
- Controlling access to data
- Cryptocurrency suspicious user alert system
- Cryptocurrency risk detection system

## Bank of New York Mellon

BNYM has a suite of patents filed largely related to the process of encryption. Their main concern appears to be to ensure that financial data is private in private networks, yet traceable. They use a private network, blockchain and cryptography to provide a block of transaction records.

## British Telecom

Mitigating a blockchain attack is at the top on their list, clearly indicating the understanding of the weaknesses of blockchain and attempting to solve for those problems.

## Cisco

Cisco has developed a suite of patents related to blockchain-based Internet of Things (IOT) devices with identity verification and anomaly detection. They've also developed a group membership on blockchain and controlling timers associated with multiple users. The connection of blockchain to devices could be a big win for Cisco down the road, when companies buy up products and license services that help them leverage the IOT and the need for verified identities to overcome serious security threats.

## Dell

Dell has a growing portfolio, including obfuscating data in a distributed ledger and commodity contracts.

## Google

Google only has one patent thus far, although is likely to have more in the works. They had a filing for a processor with external memory using blockchain and re-ordering.

## HP

This offering involves PIN verification.

## Intel

Intel also has a larger portfolio comparatively. As the maker of the processors to so many computing devices, it's not surprising they are also looking at infrastructure and how to leverage blockchain power for others. A few of the interesting patents already in the public record:

- Public key infrastructure
- Energy-efficient bitcoin mining hardware
- Accelerators for device commissioning
- Data broker-assisted transfer of device ownership
- Sequencing proof of work
- Method of scalable IOT device with onboarding capabilities

## IBM

IBM is one of the largest filers of patents to date, not surprisingly; it's number three in development. IBM has traditionally been in the top three of patent filers in the U.S. for decades, priding itself on the innovative work the company does. Building out an entire platform and looking to develop standards in the industry, a few of the patents IBM has filed include:

- Use of independent radio receivers with a single transmitter
- Clearinghouse transactions with trusted and untrusted entities
- Parallel execution of blockchain and enterprise transactions

- Personal ledger using blockchain
- Consensus-based reputation tracking in online marketplaces
- Storage adapter performance

## JP Morgan Chase

In February 2018, patents filed by JP Morgan began appearing in our tracking. Their early filings were for reconciliation of a distributed ledger related to payments (not surprisingly) and enhanced organizational transparency using a credit chain. Widely known for investing in the Ethereum Alliance and Hyperledger project, as well as many financial technology start-ups in blockchain, JP Morgan Chase will probably build rapidly its own proprietary technology in tandem with the open source projects.

## Mastercard & Visa

Mastercard and Visa both have good-sized portfolios in developing blockchain for authentication, offline verification, etc. American Express is a partner with IBM's Hyperledger, but so far does not have any of its own filings.

- Mastercard
    - Verification of identity
    - Authorization of transactions
    - Transferring trust
    - Managing offline blockchain exchanges
    - Information transaction infrastructure
    - Managing and controlling fraud in blockchain-based transactions
- Visa
    - Digital asset account management
    - Using digital signatures to create trusted digital asset transfers
    - Token check offline

## McAfee

The company widely known for scanning your computer for viruses is looking at provable traceability in blockchain. This is the type of technology needed to overcome some of the glaring concerns and potential weaknesses of blockchain.

## Microsoft

A few paces behind IBM in filings, but still with a good-size and growing portfolio, Microsoft's patents are focused on the cryptographic applications for a blockchain system. Microsoft is also working with Ethereum as part of its cloud solution. Ethereum is open source so to that extent, it can't be patented. However, Microsoft will undoubtedly build a wall around proprietary components and developments as it goes forward.

## NASDAQ

NASDAQ is clearly committed to its technology-focused business model, with several patents already filed for sharing and storing transaction data using distributed computing systems, an application framework using blockchain for asset-based ownership, and securing time-sensitive information using blockchain. Exchanging securities is sure to be affected by blockchain in the future. As speed, efficiency and security become more important, they are already one step ahead on this.

## Oracle

One of the original database companies that transformed corporations, they are also amassing a portfolio of blockchain technology that underpins how others might use it. A couple of their more interesting filings are:

- Managing scalable continuous delivery pipelines
- Encrypting data to facilitate resource savings and tamper detection

## Sales Force

Targeted to their underlying software, they have developed a messaging system that uses blockchain to ensure integrity of message delivery, which could clearly be helpful in managing a sales initiative.

## Thomson Reuters

The company serving many in the legal industry will undoubtedly have advantages if they can help their law firm customers embrace blockchain. Their filings focus on identify verification:

- Providing identity scores
- Identity creation verification and management

## Twitter

Interestingly, Twitter acquired this patent from IBM: *securing genomic information for selectively securing genetic coding regions being communicated over a network using web services.* What are they up to? Time will tell.

## Yamaha

The music company has looked at blockchain for storing and editing performance data in a performance device. This is where the management of digital rights will come in. If they are creating it at the source, it raises interesting questions about how that flows downstream through the distribution process for big media companies in the future.

## Verizon

Verizon is still in the early days of developing its portfolio, but had a patent filing to secure distributed information and password management using blockchain. Undoubtedly, this big telecom will partner with companies like IBM alongside developing its own solutions.

## Wal-mart

Interestingly, Wal-mart did not have patents filed on the highly publicized tracking of food, but rather technology clearly indicating it is preparing for head-to-head competition with Amazon. It had a patent filing for unmanned aerial delivery to a secure location — using blockchain. It also filed a patent for home delivery of prescriptions using blockchain. Wal-mart may turn out to be one of those unlikely sources of real cutting-edge use cases in the early days of blockchain emerging from the shadows of virtual currency.

The big start-up technologies are also active.

## Blockchain Technologies

As one of the early companies developing an exchange and underlying software, their patent portfolio included securely receiving and counting votes in an election, as well as a broader underlying technology tool to create multi-branched blockchain with configurable protocol rules.

## Digital Asset Holdings

One of the most highly funded fin-tech companies using blockchain, they have a good-sized portfolio with six patents in these early days, mostly focused on building the tools for clearing and settling financial transactions. These include:

- Digital asset modeling
- Asset and obligation management using flexible settlement times
- A digital asset intermediary settlement platform

## Winklevoss IP

In addition to a few trademark filings, the Winklevosses also have a few patents showing up in February 2018 for operating exchange-traded products holding digital math-based assets (i.e., cryptocurrency).

## Interesting filings in other start-ups

- Blockchain for digital media
- Monetizing digital artwork
- Multiple legal game providers across jurisdictions using blockchain
- A blockchain electronic voting system (this one dates back to 2015)
- A series of patents by different companies related to managing digital content rights, including in social media
- Monitoring a medical life cycle
- Managing health care transactions
- Coupon system using a blockchain
- Gift card transactions
- Open registry for the Internet of Things enabling users and machines to identify, authenticate and interact using blockchain

These data sets will continue to evolve, but monitoring what patents are being filed and by whom provides good marketplace indicators of the ideas being funded and what could start to shape the landscape as companies attempt to own and control various aspects of the technology. Many of these could later become standards, while some will be proprietary technology that gives the holders a competitive edge.

While many companies will opt to partner or license technologies, others have recognized early the value of developing their own portfolios. Just like the war of the smartphones pitted large corporations against each other, the battle for blockchain technology standardization and norms is already underway. Should your company be involved?

Another tool is to take a quick look at the trademarks filed using some form of the term blockchain. This helps us see how the products may be marketed in the future.

## Trademarks

There are approximately 171 live trademarks filed using the term "blockchain" in it. Only four have actually registered, all by smaller, lesser-known entities selling some form of cryptocurrency. Many would be what I classify as "trendier" trademarks of a start-up trying to find a hook using blockchain. A few examples include:

| |
|---|
| **Blockchain Fantasy Sports** |
| **Blockchain Apparel** |
| **Ethical Blockchain** |
| **Secured by Blockchain** |
| **The Blockchain of Minds** |
| **Blockchain Surfboards** |

| In Blockchain We Trust |
| --- |
| Blockchain Books |
| Gold Glory Blockchain |
| Blockchain Pub |
| Blockchain Solutions, Not Hype |
| One Blockchain at a Time |
| Green Blockchain |
| Blockchain Angels |

There are many filings for what will likely be considered descriptors, such as Blockchain Consulting, Blockchain Exchange, Blockchain Cloud, Blockchain Real Estate and so on.

Most of the filings are start-up companies. Since the term "blockchain" has already become a descriptor of the type of technology, it is likely that savvy companies will start building out more-powerful unique brands for what they are doing; however, it is helpful as a marketplace indicator to see where the trademark portfolio is at this point in time. It's largely filled with speculators trying to carve out a name for themselves in the hot new area.

**Media Coverage**

It's only been in the last year that mainstream media began more-extensive coverage of blockchain. Up until then, it was mostly sensational articles about bitcoin, the cryptocurrency that has spurred the formation of thousands of start-ups and new forms of virtual currency.

Not surprisingly, blockchain is largely misunderstood by mainstream media. The technology is hard to understand. Most of the people talking about it are technologists, so they get technical really quickly and focus on what's going to capture the attention of readers: new forms of currency, perceived wealth by those out on the forefront and then reactions by big bank leaders like Jamie Dimon.

According to the *Coin Telegraph*, widely considered the premier online publication focused on cryptocurrency, mainstream media seem to cover bitcoin or other cryptocurrency like they cover the stock market. In a January 31, 2018, interview, Tech Crunch journalist Mike Butcher opined that the "media is still playing catch up" and that even tech journalists aren't necessarily up to speed. He also said that a lot of the articles are based on well-written press releases by the blockchain companies rather than rigorous reporting.

The *Coin Telegraph* has broken its news articles into a few interesting categories that help define the state of the industry today:

- Bitcoin, Ethereum, Altcoin, Monero and Ripple all have their own categories

- Scam News (*What does this tell you?*)

- Blockchain News

- Regulation News

- Event News

If you want to really know what's happening in the blockchain world, this should be a daily check-in for you.

*Forbes* is one of the few mainstream publications that has developed a cryptocurrency market-specific beat. Most of the other major publications, like the *Wall Street Journal*, *New York Times*, *Washington Post* and other mainstream media, cover the headline-grabbing news as they come.

Over the last year, the *Wall Street Journal* had 161 articles containing the word blockchain in them, most focused on cryptocurrency, what a CIO should know, regulatory developments and which company's stock was rising based upon investments in the cutting edge space. The *Financial Times* had 853 articles containing the term blockchain, with more regular coverage of cryptocurrency. *Forbes* magazine's online version had close to 1,600 results of articles discussing blockchain or blockchain-related companies (and that's more than half of all the articles they ever wrote about blockchain since its inception in 2008).

After *Coin Telegraph*, these are likely to be your more-trusted sources of news on blockchain. Be wary of some of the general news outlets that don't have a tech-focused journalist or dedicated beat — they will likely to be more press release- or headline-driven versus real analysis.

The sources of news and information on blockchain will undoubtedly grow exponentially as big companies deploy new solutions and cryptocurrency continues to grab headlines and buzz. Of course, there are bloggers out there writing about the topic as well. Most of the start-ups have blogs and the big consulting companies are all blogging and writing about blockchain, as well as filling up You Tube channels with slick TED Talk like videos.

Just keep in mind, as you continue to read headline after headline, to separate blockchain from cryptocurrencies. They use the same underlying technologies, but their impact on business is different. Unless you are very cryptocurrency-focused, it's important to see the forest for the trees and continually question everything, but still recognize the potential long-term impact. How long will it take for blockchain to survive and change everything or fizzle out?

# 3
# THE NEXT GENERATION OF DATABASES
## *Can we predict the future from past transformations?*

Blockchain clearly has the potential to become a new underlying technology to databases and transactions throughout industries and governments in the future. While predicting the future is never an exact science, we can look historically at other shifts of a similar nature to derive guidance for what may happen and how long it may take.

In researching this shift and looking for examples in contemporary history of technologies that were underpinnings to a shift and not something consumers purchased (like smartphones or home computers), a few arise that parallel blockchain.

*[See chart next page]*

## 1960–1970s: Introduction of IBM SQL Database

## 1994: Introduction of the World Wide Web and the domain name system

## Late 1990–2000: Evolution of HTML, JAVA and other code that runs websites.

## Late 1990s–2000s: Bluetooth technology

## 1970s: Introduction of Databases and SQL standards

One of the most transformative introductions of new technology in modern times to business operation was IBM's standardization of relational databases. This introduction was the foundation to the information age and transactions we all experience today, such as bank deposits, credit card purchases and online auctions, to name just a few. Many of you may recall experiencing this transformation in the early days of your career.

According to company archives, IBM introduced FORTRAN (formula translation), a computer language based on algebra, grammar and syntax rules, as far back as the 1950s. It would become the most widely used computer languages for a technical network at the time. IBM continued its development of FORTRAN and created the SQL database in the 1970s, which would later become a standard to computer and database operations that changed everything. IBM was not the only company, though, developing technology that would become a future standard for how nearly all companies operated.

Akin to IBM, according to Oracle's company archives, Relational Software (now Oracle) became the standard for relational database management systems after IBM developed the language structure English query language (SEQUEL or SQL), introducing the first commercially available implementation of SQL in 1979. By 1986, nearly a decade after IBM invented SQL, the American National Standards Institute (ANSI) standardized SQL. Thereafter, all major relational databases supported this standard. By the late 1980s, the International Standards Organization (ISO) also named SQL as the standard for relational databases.

This is important in considering blockchain because it helps us recognize that it took nearly two decades from the formation of IBM's FORTRAN and SQL to transform business operations through the 1980s and beyond. Of course, during these two decades, a few other technology companies were forming right alongside this standardization of databases and contributing to the global information technology age. They created the companies, the hardware and the software that would be needed to propel us into the information age: Microsoft, Sun Microsystems, Cisco, Texas Instruments, Hughes Net, Hewlett Packard, to name just a few.

This evolution into the relational database driven by SQL language was the very foundation of how companies evolved from manually tracking information by hand to large-scale software and relational databases transforming how transactions and information was maintained. Over time, this evolved to web- and cloud-based client/server environments, but the formation of SQL is an important historical indicator because it demonstrates how this new language is created, then standardized and fully adopted into business operations. SQL is a language, much like blockchain is a type of language operating behind the scenes.

It took nearly two decades for SQL to become a standard operating system in business and government. Will it take as long for blockchain to become a standard? Or will the accelerating pace of change also apply to this potential disruptor of how we currently manage databases and transactions?

The next paradigm shift in our recent history was the introduction of the world wide web and domain name system. It most closely parallels what could happen with blockchain. Many of you may not be familiar with how it all happened, so let's take a deeper look at how long that took to become standardized.

## 1994: Introduction of the World Wide Web and the domain name system

By the early 1990s, the internet was morphing from a primarily academic and government-accessible communication tool to mainstream opportunities for businesses and individuals. To understand how the internet actually came to be, it's helpful to look at the root systems and the formation of the domain name system. I'll try to keep this at a very high level, but it is instructive in looking at how blockchain could also become a distributed network that we all use.

A couple of components power the internet as we know it today: a decentralized system of name servers, powered by numbers but interpreted by names we can remember through web browsers. You don't realize all that's going on when you type in Amazon.com. I go into a lot of detail about the history here, because I think it is most on point with what could happen in blockchain.

According to the National Academic Press, the domain name system was designed and deployed in the 1980s to overcome technical and operational constraints of the prior *hosts.txt* system of connecting computers in different locations. This is a relevant comparison because in these early days, only academicians and government workers had access to this system, much like only technologists can access the popular blockchain platforms today. Originally referred to as ARPANET, registration of hosts (i.e., computer nodes) and distribution of information needed to keep it current (i.e., connecting points) were managed by the Network Information Center at Stanford Research Institute. As ARPANET began to grow in use, still in a very niched manner, it became clear that the *hosts.txt* method of sharing information was not going to continue to work at a scaled level. The domain name system would have to allow for the scale of this kind of computerized information sharing. This same scale is needed for blockchain to succeed.

By the early 1980s, Zwu-Sing Su and Jon Postel published the report "The Domain Name Convention for Internet User Applications," which described how internet naming should be changed to facilitate a distributed name system. They envisioned organizing names into hierarchies represented by text- or word-based components separated by a period or dot (i.e., google.com, etc.). They designed a complex root zone with directories to create the beginning concept of the infrastructure of today's domain name system. For example, today, you may think of dot-com or dot.org as the root zone of the internet and Amazon.com or Tiffany.com as a domain name in the root zone of dot.com.

Like blockchain, the DNS — domain name system — is based upon nodes or end points in the system with the various levels of the domain names. Essentially, though, a domain name is just a text form of directing a computer to a specific IP (internet protocol) address or string of numbers. Humans are much more capable of recognizing or memorizing names than a long string of numbers. This was the underlying concept of how to make it easier to connect all of these computers. For the consumer, however, to access a website or a domain name, applications such as web browsers or e-mail software would be required. The initial construct was for a uniform resource identifier (i.e., http://www.google.com) to direct the user experience to a specific place on the internet. A series of name servers at each of the nodes in the hierarchy then implement the DNS.

I don't want to go too much deeper into the technical world of how the internet works at the risk of losing sight of the historical comparison and remaining appropriately in layman's terms, but the similarities are here and a little bit of detail is instructive. The bottom line is within the structure of the domain name system that exists today, there are multiple root name servers to distribute the query workload and ensure reliable operations.

This is not very different from how blockchain runs between nodes or the purpose of the distribution (decentralized ledger), which is to ensure not only reliable operations, but certainty and trust in the information encoded into each block between the nodes.

To function on the internet, a computer must have some basic information, such as its IP address and the IP address of at least one router and a few critical services.

As the DNS became standardized, another important and related trend was occurring. According to the Current Population Survey (conducted by the U.S. Census Bureau), personal computer adoption in the United States continued to increase throughout the 1990s and demonstrated a five-fold increase from 1984. By the year 2000, 51 percent, or 54 million households, had access to at least one computer at home, up from 36.6 percent in 1997. The percentage of households with Internet access more than doubled between these years, from 18 percent in 1997 to 41.5 percent, or 42 million households, by the year 2000. Computer access and Internet access were becoming synonymous: More than four in five households with computer access also had internet access.

Sometime around 1996 or 1997, browser manufacturers made dot-com the default value for any names typed directly into the browser command line. That is, whenever a user typed <name> without a top-level domain into the command line, the browser automatically directed the user to www.<name>.com. Making dot-com the default value for all browser entries reinforced the value of dot-com registrations relative to other top level domains (i.e., dot.org, dot.net, etc). In effect, a dot.com domain name functioned as a global keyword, and the possession of a common, simple word in the dot.com space was sure to generate significant traffic from web browsers.

This explains, to some degree, why some domain names sold for hundreds of thousands or even millions of dollars. The scarcity drove up value and for marketers, this default for consumers made dot-com addresses the gold standard, which continues today despite thousands of other top-level domains being available.

This is relevant because as blockchain evolves, we must watch for how consumer adoption of the concept and/or adoption of new assets of value is driven by the companies developing the tools, devices and interface with which we access this new underlying technology.

For example, will our desire for privacy and security, combined with the rapidly evolving Internet of Things and artificial intelligence technology, mean that some form of blockchain will become a default setting? Or will one blockchain platform earn our trust as consumers more than another, so we want to know what brand of blockchain is inside the devices that connect our life?

I often use a clip from the "Today Show" in 1994 (http://www.boardroom.solutions/inside-the-book ) where then-hosts Katie Couric and Bryant Gumble discuss what this thing called the internet is. Today, we are at that same point. Outside a select number of people who are in the blockchain business, most people today are saying, "What is this blockchain thing?" How much time will pass before blockchain disrupts our world the way the internet did? Will it disrupt at the magnitude and profound level from where we were in 1994? Will there be a blockchain bubble and bust?

Before departing from the history of the internet, it's helpful to look at a couple of other components.

In a recent *Harvard Business Review* article, authors Marco Iansiti and Karim R. Lakhani noted the similarities in the adoption of TCP/IP protocols. This is also the underlying technology behind the domain name system. There are a few important points to consider from their study:

- Introduced in 1972, TCP/IP (Transmission Control Protocol and Internet Protocol — the standards to connect computers) first gained traction in the U.S. Department of Defense. To become commercial, telecom service providers and equipment manufactures had to invest billions in building dedicated lines and technology infrastructure. Many were initially skeptical about the new internet protocol. Few imagined what would come of connecting the world. By the late 1980s, companies like Sun, NeXT, HP and Silicon Graphics created localized private networks. They created the building blocks and in the 1990s, it exploded.

- Blockchain is a new peer-to-peer network that sits on top of the internet. Introduced originally in 2008 for bitcoin, it is evolving and could follow a path similar to the TCP/IP evolution. It could become the new system of record for all transactions. If so, the economy will once again undergo a radical shift as new, blockchain-based sources influence and control.

- The ledger is replicated in a large number of identical databases, each hosted and maintained by an interested party. When charges are entered in one copy, all the other copies are simultaneously updated. This reconciliation should be able to be settled within seconds, securely and verifiability.

- There are two similar components to the adoption of blockchain: novelty and complexity. The more novel and complex something is, the more it takes for the masses to understand and adopt it. Clearly, blockchain is novel and complex; therefore, it will take time for adoption. Two dimensions affect how technology evolves.

- According to the authors, the easiest place to start will be single-use applications such as adding digital currency as a payment mechanism or evaluating internal databases for managing physical and digital addresses or verifying identities.

In the 1990s, as the commercial interest in domain names began to grow and usage of the internet became more mainstream, it was clear that some standardization and governance would be required. The Network Information Center mentioned earlier in the formation of the domain name system had been managed by the U.S. Department of Defense and was subcontracted out to Network Solutions, Inc. in 1992. The National Science Foundation replaced the Department of Defense as the funding source for the Network Information Center, powering the emerging World Wide Web and engaged Network Solutions to take over domain name registration services for most of the top-level domains through a five-year agreement.

By 1998, the National Science Foundation transferred authority to the U.S. Department of Commerce. Led by Jon Postel, an international group of constituencies formed the governance principles and set out the bylaws of ICANN, which was formed in 1998. It was at this time that the basic structure of the internet began to form with the separation of registrar (i.e., like a GoDaddy) and registry operations (i.e., like Verisign contracting to run dot.com) and that no changes to the root zone of the internet would occur without permission of the U.S. government (until 2016, however, when the Obama administration relinquished this control to ICANN as an independent global organization).

Alongside the formation of ICANN as the governing body to direct policy for the domain name system, the Internet Engineering Task Force was formed as a voluntary, non-commercial organization comprising individuals concerned with the evolution of the architecture and operation of the internet. While participation was and is open to anyone, participants are largely technologists from universities, network infrastructure operators and companies in related industries (that is, it is very technical).

The internet continues to be governed by ICANN, with the IANA (Internet Assigned Numbers Authority) administering all of the names and numbers and the root zone of the internet under the authority of ICANN and the IETF setting technical standards and best practices for the back-end operation of the internet.

Not surprisingly, as the underlying technology and protocols governing the internet connected the world commercially, industries were adopting and changing at the same time. Consider how the financial sector exploded with the advent of e-trade and the ability to now manage your account finances, stocks and accounting online. This would lead to a revolution in the financial industry as it turned into a 24–7 news cycle, with market reactions often being technology-driven through algorithms or fear, driven by humans with the ability to transact their own business online immediately.

Likewise, the network infrastructure that would be required was identified by big telecommunications companies. Verizon, AT&T, Time Warner, Comcast and others invested billions in the last mile of deploying broadband and connectivity. Cellphone towers and wireless networks were installed as the infrastructure of the world in which we live today was created. This is also relevant because today's debate over net neutrality poses the question of whether those companies who invested in creating that infrastructure should now be regulated and required to provide equal access, or whether they should be able to charge what the market will bear from the companies pumping out content using their bandwidth.

What similar investments are being made today by companies that could later be subject to regulation? What infrastructure will be needed to scale blockchain? What standard and norms will be needed to connect a group of decentralized computers and then give consumers access to it in some trusted way? What investments are needed for blockchain to transform our world? If you are considering how blockchain will affect your business, don't underestimate this comparison — think about the possibilities at a deeper level.

One final point on the evolution of the internet and domain name system. In 2012, ICANN created a program for new top-level domains to be introduced to the root zone of the internet. Many companies and financial institutions, like Barclays, JP Morgan, PNC,

Visa, American Express, Prudential, Capital One, Citi, BB&T, Discovery, Northwestern, AIG and others, acquired their own access to the root zone of the internet. They have full control over these spaces. It's quite possible that these new spaces could become a key to the companies leveraging the underlying blockchain technology.

Much like the earlier example of AXA insurance using FIZZY.AXA as its portal for consumer access to the blockchain, financial and other companies could build out blockchain solutions in their own root zones of the internet, accessed by traditional browsers.

Some of the existing blockchain networks have created their own alternate root zones. They operate under Dot Bit or Dot Eth – Ethereum or Dot Coin. This means they are operating their own internet-based systems. To access it requires specific software rather than just a traditional web browser. It also means a lot of infrastructure will have to be created to connect their blockchains to everyone. These new top-level domains are already part of the existing domain name system, but operating at the root zone of the internet and accessible via a traditional web browser. The new financial top-level domains such as Dot Insurance and Dot Bank, which are closed for exclusive access to those industries, can use the root zone that is accessible by consumers to deliver blockchain-based products.

I'll pick up on this again in Chapter Five with practical steps, but for now, recognize that the introduction of the domain name system, TCP/IP protocols, the investment of infrastructure by telecommunications companies and the governing body of ICANN were critical to the digital revolution we have all experienced in the last decade or two.

In terms of timing, ICANN was formed in 1998. It's been 20 years. It took about 10 for the revolution to fully take shape, so even in recent examples, we are seeing a long window for transformation. The question looms: Do you want to wait and let others lead the transformation, or do you want to take part in it? What lessons can we learn from prior failures?

## Late 1990–2000: Evolution of HTML, JAVA and other code that runs websites

As the internet became a staple of the new marketing strategies of companies in the late nineties and early 2000s, the underlying code language used to create these online experiences we know so well today would also change dramatically. Just as you don't have to understand how HTML (hypertext markup language) or JAVA (a programming language) works to use a website, you won't ever really need to understand how blockchain works to know what it can do. Let's take a quick look at how Java was introduced and how long it took to become mainstream.

Java was introduced in 1995. Because of Java, we expect digital devices to be smarter, more functional and way more entertaining. In short, your digital experiences would be vastly different without Java. In 1991, a small group of Sun engineers called the Green Team believed that the next wave in computing was the union of digital consumer devices and computers. Led by James Gosling, the team worked around the clock and created the programming language that would revolutionize our world: Java. The Green Team demonstrated the new language with an interactive, handheld home entertainment controller that originally targeted the digital cable television industry. Unfortunately, the concept was much too advanced for the team at the time — but it was just right for the Internet. In 1995, the team announced that the Netscape Navigator Internet browser would incorporate Java technology.

Today, Java is the underlying technology for many of the applications and devices that power our day-to-day lives.

According to Java historians, five goals were taken into consideration while developing Java:

- Keep it simple, familiar and object-oriented.

- Keep it robust and secure.

- Keep it architecture-neutral and portable.

- Make it executable with high performance.

- Ensure it is interpreted, threaded and dynamic.

Java is implemented over a number of places in the modern world. It is implemented as a standalone application, web application, enterprise application and mobile application for games, smart cards, embedded systems, robotics, desktops, etc. Java is used for mobile phones, point-of-sale systems, video games, trading applications and Big Data technologies.

Java underpins most of what we do today, yet few people, other than developers, recognize that reality. Java was created in the early 1990s and became open source in 2006. This meant the technology could be deployed at a scaled and faster pace — but that was nearly 10 years after it was introduced. What's different at the early stages of blockchain is that it is already open source. The big developers have made it open source, so it can grow, develop and become more-secure and scalable faster. This could accelerate the timeline we have seen in these early introductions of game-changing technology. What we can learn from Java, however, is that these underlying technologies, when standardized and leveraged by many companies at once, have the power to transform many facets of business across industries.

## 1990s–2000s: Bluetooth technology

Bluetooth is another technology that we now take for granted every time we connect a device wirelessly to a speaker, a television, headphones, etc., but think little about how it evolved.

You don't go out and buy Bluetooth — it simply comes on your devices, much like you probably won't go out and buy blockchain as a consumer, but rather use it embedded into applications and devices in the future such as Internet of Things, Smart Home, Smart Cars, etc.

In 1994, Ericsson, the Swedish telecommunications company, developed the idea of replacing the tangle of RS-232 cables that were commonly used to communicate between devices with a wireless alternative. Other companies, including Intel and Nokia, had also developed wireless concepts of cellphones and computers. These companies recognized that for universal interoperability, the technology would need standardization. They formed a Special Interest Group (SIG) and in 1996, agreed to form their group to create that standardized wireless technology that we all rely on today. The Bluetooth Special Interest Group was officially formed by Ericsson, Nokia, Intel, Toshiba and IBM.

In 1998, a first version was launched. By 2005, Version 2.0 was ratified by the group, which now had 4,000 members. In June of 2007, the Bluetooth SIG acquired Wibree Alliance, a Nokia-led initiative that included Nordic Semiconductor, which had developed a low-power form of wireless connectivity that would work with cellphones. Today, Bluetooth technology is incorporated into billions of chips in thousands of applications and extends to continuing new sectors of devices, including now the Internet of Things. The SIG has more than 30,000 members. The Hyperledger Project and Ethereum Alliance are similar to the SIG.

It took well over a decade before Bluetooth became something any consumer had heard of, but it would never be a product they bought. It was not until the smartphone in 2007 that the average consumer would even know the name.

What is most relevant in the comparison to blockchain is that the companies developing similar wireless concepts quickly recognized that for any Bluetooth-like technology to be scaled and deployed around the world, standardization and protocols would be required. Rather than allowing government to step in (such as how the domain name system was formed), they quickly created their own interest group to drive the technology.

IBM has clearly taken that leading step again in the formation of its Hyperledger project to drive standardization of blockchain. Because of the implications of blockchain in government transactions, it is likely that more standardization could be required than that for Bluetooth.

As you consider these examples of how a technology or concept was developed and what steps were taken to standardize it and create the products, software and network required to leverage its power, we can derive predictions about what could happen with blockchain.

Blockchain will not be something a consumer buys, but they will come to recognize it as something they trust, like the branded "Intel Inside."

What is clear from all of these examples is that it is often a 10- to 15-year cycle from when technology is first invented to when it settles into a staple of technology and society. Blockchain was first introduced in 2008. We are clearly in these early formation days, but also nearing a tipping point of development where standardization will be formed and then scale can occur.

In the next chapter, I detail what will be needed for blockchain to become a standard underlying technology and touch on the cryptocurrency component in all of this. I'd like to close this chapter by looking again at what functions blockchain could transform in society and recognize that many of these cross over to corporations, financial institutions, infrastructure and government.

## Industries to be Affected

As we look at these parallel transformations and consider the benefits of using blockchain in transaction, once again, study the industries and functions that could be affected..

**Financial Services**

- Letters of credit
- Cross-currency payments
- Mortgages
- Processing transactions

**Government**

- Land registry and ownership
- Vehicle registry and ownership
- Citizen identification

**Healthcare**

- Medical records
- Pharmaceutical supply & tracking

**Insurance**

- Claims processing
- Internet of Things integration for policy monitoring

**Manufacturing**

- Supply chain tracking
- Products, parts & logistics tracking
- Maintenance records
- Internet of Things

**Food Supply**

- From farm to table

**Media**

- Digital rights in music, movies, photographs, trademarks and intellectual property

# 4
# WHAT BLOCKCHAIN NEEDS TO CHANGE THE WAY WE DO BUSINESS

Technologists still have a number of concerns about using blockchain for critical functions in our society, not to mention protocols, governance, laws and regulations that will all have to be addressed. I've outlined just a few of the more high-level ones here for consideration.

As you evaluate blockchain in your own organization, consider whether your company should invest in resources to help lead and pave the way in creating these new protocols and regulations.

Some of the big roadblocks blockchain faces are:

- It's a solution looking for a problem. Blockchain emerged as the bitcoin currency. Then everyone got all excited about it and started looking at the potential versus creating blockchain to solve a problem.

- It's not easy to access for end users. This isn't like HTML, where a user can gain access to an existing web browser. Technology to get an end user to access the blockchain is needed. This inherently means some other types of systems will be needed.

- Will it actually decrease or increase transaction costs? While the "smart contract" component of blockchain promises to reduce layers of bureaucracy and processing, some argue that the cost savings are dubious. "Moving cash equity markets to a blockchain infrastructure would drive a significant increase of the overall transaction costs," said Axel Pierron, founding and managing director of the financial consulting firm Optimas LLC, in a 2017 *Forbes* article. Additionally, his concern that mistakes could be irreversible could result in significant losses.

- Blockchain requires enough parties using the same implementation of the technology. Without universal adoption, the benefits of blockchain cannot be realized.

- Blockchain is too complicated. Every article out there that attempts to explain how blockchain works usually leaves readers more confused than enlightened. If people can't understand it, how will they use it and adopt it?

- Performance could be unreliable. Because of their distributed nature, blockchain transactions can only complete when all parties update their ledgers, which could take hours — this is why standardization and governance will become so important.

- The fact that a blockchain transaction cannot be changed may not be a good thing and may not be compatible with the latest privacy laws. This is why governance and development will be required. It might not be worldwide, but more country-specific, because of this reason.

- To use blockchain will require that parallel systems continue to operate. This could undermine the cost savings or reduce the return on investment, rendering the benefits unattainable.

- Some believe blockchain is really just a Trojan horse to undermine the global financial system. This fear could overshadow development.

According to a *Forbes* article, five issues prevent blockchain from going mainstream:

- **Scalability**. The current limit for Ethereum is 15 transactions per second. This will have to speed up exponentially to allow for the billions of transactions occurring each day.

- **Interoperability**. A number of blockchains are addressing the interoperability issue – ICOM, AIOn and WANCHAIN, which founded the Interoperability Alliance. The goal is connecting blockchain protocols.

- **Privacy**. The built-in anonymity could be a good and bad thing. It's a good thing in a world where privacy is valued and protected in some parts of the world. It's a bad thing when the bad actors can hide in the shadows and potentially hack, steal and thwart legitimate law enforcement efforts.

- **Regulations**. Embracing regulation will be required to prevent crime and abuses (see more below on the DAO attack).

- **Governance**. To transact anything of value, most individuals want to feel a sense of trust. To garner trust, some type of governing body or trusted organization is needed.

I've broken all of these challenges into a few basic categories:
- Governance and Regulation
- Connectivity, Standards & Infrastructure
- Acceptance & Trust
- The Currency Conundrum

## Governance & Regulation

The root purpose of regulation is to prevent bad human behavior intended to put corporate profits over the greater good and to provide some rule or framework from which to operate. Blockchain is intended to improve the way transactions are managed and stored. Whether it's currency, the copyright to a song or transferring your home at closing, blockchain has to have some basic rules for society to embrace it.

Many proponents of blockchain believe that it is able to overcome the "bad actor" in humans and prevent humans from stealing. However good the technology, though, humans are always part of the equation. Let's take the example of the DAO attack.

## *The DAO Attack – humans are always part of the equation*

As much as blockchain purports to solve human-related problems in transactions, the problem may simply be that humans can never be fully removed from the process. The smart contract component of blockchain is one of its most alluring for broader business purposes. The coding of the series of *if-then algorithmic events* is built into the contract itself, eliminating many steps in a process and reducing the need for humans. However, in the case of DAO (Decentralized Autonomous Organization — a digital currency exchange), hackers made off with $50 million in virtual currency. DAO was supposed to be a way of decentralizing an investment fund. Instead of a few partners deciding which companies to invest in, the members of the fund made the decisions.

The more you contributed, the more weight your voted carried. The distributed nature of the fund meant no one could run off with the money.

DAO is built on Ethereum. The idea was to have more democracy in the financial institution. Each unit of Ether (the currency of Ethereum) is unique and traceable. DAO says if the hacker tries to sell the stolen Ether, the system will flag it. It turns out, though, there may have been a mistake in the code that allowed a hacker to run a transaction, withdrawing funds before the system realized it was happening. Through that weakness in the code, the hacker was able to steal millions of "dollars" in Ether. As explained in *Wired* magazine, the DAO team could solve the problem simply by recreating what existed before the hack, ostensibly turning back the clock to before the hack.

This, however, raises the very concerns that so many have about cryptocurrencies and blockchain in general. If it can all be rigged and manipulated like this, how can anyone trust it? Doesn't that create a bigger problem than the technology is trying to solve?

This conundrum, like many others, will have to be solved for blockchain to truly transform our world as it claims it can. Wherever this kind of manipulation can occur, rules and governance principles will be needed.

Imagine, for example, if a county recorder's office could simply turn back the clock on real estate transactions and undo the sale of a building or a home because someone of great influence wanted it. How could anyone rely on this as a clearinghouse for transactions of such importance? Some governing body or structure with a clear set of rules and accountability will be required for people to trust clearinghouses for transactions and property.

Consider the evolution of the domain name system. To connect the world through a distributed set of servers and ensure consistent results, the domain name system was needed to connect everything technically. Then governing principles and policies were required, which is why ICANN was created. Global policy was needed to connect a worldwide set of computers in a way that protected rights across borders, laws and cultures.

But is the same needed here? Could industries simply solve these problems the way SQL databases and Oracle evolved into a standard operating system, or the way Java or HTML was formed and evolved into open source? Does blockchain really require a worldwide governing organization to determine how it operates?

Most likely, the answer is in how our current system operates. For global transactions, some form of acceptance of value and government-backed currency is required, but exchanges operate by their own rules and different countries have different laws and regulations governed by their own agencies. While our current systems could implement blockchain technology, it would be within the existing framework and set of rules.

Some believe the value of blockchain is that it can transcend these traditional roadblocks or boundary lines, while others are concerned about that as a serious threat.

As the technology develops further, the question of what type of governance is required undoubtedly will equally evolve. Many companies and groups are attempting to solve this problem. The list is too long to even begin to cover — IBM is at the forefront, but many universities and academics around the world are also jumping into the discussion, along with the big consulting companies like Deloitte and PWC vying for a seat at the table as these new governing principles are developed. Additionally, the organizations that traditionally lead the formation of standards like the ISO are forming committees to address this issue.

There are probably hundreds, if not thousands, of groups discussing and trying to form governance-based solutions to this question right now. But how will any one government, let alone the world, agree upon a single standard or framework? How will these complex issues be resolved? Will the industry that has quickly formed around it backed by big companies self-regulate and create it? Will an intergovernmental organization like ICANN form to create a stakeholder-based model? Or will the marketplace weed out the weak companies and ideas in favor of a more-predominant, scalable model? Will you be a part of the discussion or just wait and see what happens?

## Connectivity, Standards, & Infrastructure

The very nature of a blockchain requires that it exist between multiple computer nodes and a set of parties who verify the information loaded into the ledger and into the block. Blockchain has to exist in an eco system. Will a new system be created or will it work within the existing internet domain name system? Will new software be developed? How will it connect the Internet of Things in remote devices?

In looking at the parallel histories of Java and Bluetooth, this appears to be the easier of the problems to overcome. A group of companies and thought leaders coming together to collaborate and find the ways for blockchain to become standardized is clearly needed. As I mentioned, Hyperledger and Ethereum are already leading the way in creating these connectivity standards as open source to allow for rapid scalability, but many universities are also working to address these pressing issues, perhaps in more of a stealth mode, and many companies are building out proprietary components of their intended blockchain use by patenting the technology.

Which of these platforms or communities will emerge as the SIG that was used for Bluetooth or be adopted by the ISO or ANSI as a standard?

Many developer communities have already been forming to support the emergence of blockchain technology. Companies will start hiring engineers and technology executives who understand the capabilities and how to overcome the challenges: How will blockchain overcome the scalability issues? What additional network infrastructure between organizations will be needed? Which companies will provide that infrastructure? How will they profit from their investments in these spaces?

How will companies transition from existing systems to newer systems using blockchain? How long will that take? This is probably the biggest looming question to consider. It's easy to recognize that new forms of currency could suddenly emerge on a blockchain — why not? It didn't exist before. Take the example of AXA's insurance product, Fizzy. That product was a new launch and a fairly short-lived transaction (travel insurance on a specific flight). Once that flight is complete, the transaction is over. This is not overly complicated to launch with blockchain because if a problem does occur, it can be corrected — and what are the consequences? A few hundred dollars per transaction?

When you start to consider connecting worldwide financial systems, insurance, land records, or even citizenship, though — going to the essence of identity in a modern world — the risks become a lot greater. How do you migrate from one system to a wholly new one? Do you have to run them in parallel for a period of time? How long? Even if the technology works, it's not an easy matter and many remain skeptical about how well it will actually work.

As hacks of cryptocurrency exchanges continue, it's unlikely governments and financial institutions will simply abandon centralizing their authority in maintaining customer information. This is not entirely unlike the Y2K concerns of old-school databases that had not prepared for the turn of the century. How do you take existing relational databases that are running and operating most of the world's systems and transition them to this untested new technology? Without clear operability standards, proven use cases and clear laws that will govern those transactions, none of that can possibly occur.

Who will make money in all of this and why is it driving up the stock price of any company that suddenly adds blockchain to its name or list of product offerings? These are the questions to consider as you look at who will lead the standardization of blockchain into the various facets of our society it purports to improve.

If the ledger can't be changed unless the parties agree to it, how do companies manage that balance of power with consumers? How are consumers protected? What liability exists? Who will insure those types of exposures? There is a vast, long list of legal and risk management complications reaching far beyond only the technology needed to consider implementing blockchain. Clearly, there are more questions than answers, but we have to start with the questions to begin to create a roadmap of how blockchain scales and integrates into these functions.

What remains clear is that the technology has to actually work and prove out the business case: that blockchain solves real problems. That requires these leaders find the technical solutions to connectivity and standardization. However, if you are in the business of building or using databases, handling transactions, tracking supplies, verifying identities, managing digital rights, or providing solutions and services to those activities, etc. (i.e., pretty much every business), you may not want to simply sit on the sidelines.

Companies that will make money from the blockchain investment are not unlike the early development of Verizon, Time Warner, Comcast and others evolving into the internet age. Some type of connectivity is going to be required — what system will that be? Is it something that already exists or can connect to, or will an entirely new system be needed?

Some type of centralization of blockchain protocols will be required. If that is developed, could it be scaled and licensed to users? As blockchain develops, there are tremendous areas of opportunity alongside the risks. As you consider your role in the standardization, carefully evaluate the opportunities that exist for your business – it could change everything.

## Acceptance & Trust

It took 10 or more years for the internet to be fully accepted and trusted by businesses as a new way of doing business and ultimately nearly two decades to transform our society. So, too, does blockchain have a long road ahead to full integration into our business, government and societal systems.

The fact that blockchain has started with a bang as the underpinnings to bitcoin and new cryptocurrency could actually do more harm than good. It has quickly become synonymous with what many believe to be fraudulent, illegitimate or "get rich quick" schemes. In my travels, I continually overhear the hype of slick-looking guys in airport lounges loudly talking up how rich they are in bitcoin. As individual investors report big gains, the interest remains high but so does the skepticism.

Additionally, blockchain is difficult to understand. Even starting with the term "distributed ledger" throws most people off and turns them off. Part of the problem is that most of the people who deeply understand blockchain are so "in the weeds" that it's hard to speak to people who don't have a clue what any of it means. It's complicated, it's new and it seems to be part of something that's less than credible. That creates a lot of problems that blockchain will have to overcome in earning trust in the boardroom and in the mind of the consumer.

The more-trusted and well-known companies and brands promote their blockchain products and projects. The more education is provided for executives across the organization in a nontechnical manner, the faster blockchain can begin to overcome the initial concerns of corporate and government leaders, but convincing the court of public opinion of those individuals who will ultimately use blockchain may take a strategic and concerted effort.

Even Bluetooth, which did not have these same challenges, had a long road for people to understand how it was useful in their life. This will be the big question to answer: "Why do I care – why does this matter for me? Do I trust it?" Before companies transition their existing operations and certainly before any government would move management of government records, the public will have to embrace and accept blockchain as trusted.

It's going to take more than a few stories in the *Wall Street Journal*. This is a long-term effort. Companies with a vested interest in blockchain futures should be investing in education and evangelism along with the technological developments required, as well as carefully educating their boards of directors, top executives and consumers.

## The Currency Conundrum

*One Man's Trash*
*is Another Man's Treasure*

Currency has value because governments, businesses and institutions agree on its value to exchange things we want or need. But is that really the only way it can work?

There is a whole "Second Life" out there on the internet, where you can build businesses and have a life in a strictly digital world. They refer to their currency as "linden dollars." It has value within that world, but can't be turned into government backed currency, so how valuable is it? In fact, some have posted about how they moved their Second Life linden dollars into bitcoin to try to find a way to convert them to real money they can use outside second life.

Video games also have currency, sometimes referred to as a Loot Box, where you can pay U.S. dollars for stuff in the game or you can earn stuff in the game and then trade with the game currency.

Blockchain could revolutionize our world with the current regulated currencies, but what has emerged so quickly at its beginning are virtual currencies not sponsored or backed by a government. This raises so many questions philosophically and politically about what currency will mean in the future. Are we at a tipping point where government-backed securities lose their value?

If you say you are a bitcoin billionaire — what does that really mean? We all hear about someone being worth x number of dollars on paper, but if they can't use that to buy a bigger house, pay for a child's education, buy groceries or set it aside for the future, what's it really worth? Is the stock market any different? The market is up 10% today, but unless you sell your stock, are you 10% richer?

Virtual currencies are assigned values by those playing the game, so to speak, but until they can trade that currency for something like food, shelter, clothing, a luxury item or a hotel room, what value does it really have? Some hotels, restaurants and retailers have begun to accept various forms of cryptocurrency, which begins to change how you look at this issue.

Some of these companies have started to launch Initial Coin Offerings (ICOs) of their virtual currencies where they sell "coins" for actual dollars. The SEC has determined this is like any other offering or privately held interest in a company; the investors must be accredited and receive certain disclosures. Is it really any different from investing in a start-up company? I've personally invested (dollars) in a number of start-ups. The money goes to pay for things you need, like hiring people and investing in software and technology or marketing costs. However, nine out of 10 start-up companies fail completely, so the money is totally lost.

What's the difference in investing in that versus some virtual currency? If the company succeeded, it might be sold and then broken into a lot of pieces or just taken out of the marketplace. Why all the concern about ICOs?

Initial Coin Offerings will continue, not unlike a lot of start-ups that raised insane amounts of capital in the dot-com bubble promising to revolutionize the world. The similarities between the two transformations, separated by 20 years of dramatic technological change, are there — whether you believe the same thing will occur is up to you.

As a sidebar, in the U.S., ICOs are currently handled the same way as a start-up. This means that "investors" in the new "coin" or shares of the company have to be accredited investors (i.e., earning at least $200,000 per year or with a net worth of at least $1 million). There are important disclosure documents and filings in the state and possibly with the SEC, but it's really not all that different. For now, "coin" is no different from shares of a privately held corporation or interest of a limited liability company: merely a term of art for people investing in what they hope will be the next big thing, with a payoff at the end. Like start-ups, most will fail, but some may pave the way for a new form of currency.

In December of 2017, Jay Clayton, chair of the SEC, posted an advisory on initial coin offerings. He clearly warned investors that initial coin offerings are not listed with the SEC and to be wary of any ICO that states it is registered with the SEC. He recognizes that whether these are classified as private securities or not, they can be an effective way for entrepreneurs to raise funds for their activities. However, he offers guidance on those investments, saying they require the proper disclosures and verifications that the investor is a qualified investor.

Many of these ICOs are clearly not following this guidance and could later be subject to lawsuits and liability from the government. They argue that they are offering a coin or a token that is not a security, but that argument will hinge on details that are still being evaluated by regulators and for which we have yet to see legislation or lawsuits. All of this means ICOs should be evaluated carefully. The SEC advises a few critical questions for any ICO:

- Who exactly am I contracting with?
  - Who is issuing and sponsoring the product, what are their backgrounds, and have they provided a full and complete description of the product? Do they have a clear written business plan that I understand?
  - Who is promoting or marketing the product, what are their backgrounds, and are they licensed to sell the product? Have they been paid to promote the product?
  - Where is the enterprise located?
- Where is my money going and what will it be used for? Is my money going to be used to "cash out" others?
- What specific rights come with my investment?
- Are there financial statements? If so, are they audited, and by whom?
- Are there trading data? If so, is there some way to verify those data?
- How, when and at what cost can I sell my investment? For example, do I have a right to give the token or coin back to the company or to receive a refund? Can I resell the coin or token, and if so, are there any limitations on my ability to resell?
- If a digital wallet is involved, what happens if I lose the key? Will I still have access to my investment?
- If a blockchain is used, is the blockchain open and public? Has the code been published, and has there been an independent cybersecurity audit?

- Has the offering been structured to comply with the securities laws and if not, what implications will that have for the stability of the enterprise and the value of my investment?

- What legal protections may or may not be available in the event of fraud, a hack, malware or a downturn in business prospects? Who will be responsible for refunding my investment if something goes wrong?

- If I do have legal rights, can I enforce them effectively and will there be adequate funds to compensate me if my rights are violated?

Of course, the other big agency to look at cryptocurrency is the IRS. How is it taxed? Right now, the IRS treats cryptocurrencies as an asset or property, so transactions are subject to capital gains taxes. This reinforces the SEC position that cryptocurrency is like buying private securities or stock.

As blockchain continues its technological evolution, governments will undoubtedly begin to tackle virtual currency and how it fits in the existing framework. Would the world ever come to one global currency? This is unlikely in the near future.

If we look at how the internet is governed today, we can already see that despite having an organization like ICANN to control the domain name system and use a bottom-up policy-making process, various governments still set their own rules. The European Union is introducing intensive privacy legislation for how companies conduct business on the internet — known as General Data Protection Regulation (GDPR). China, infamously, blocks many internet sites for its citizens. Other countries block content they do not want their citizens to see. Governments still control their own internets.

The same is likely to continue for currency, but could there be some global identification means using blockchain that countries accept for admittance to other countries? Could other global transactions become accepted by businesses everywhere, thereby threatening the value of government-backed securities? Will businesses and individuals transcend these rules and frameworks? These are all true possibilities with blockchain.

There are, obviously, more questions than answers, but the first step to breaking down a checklist of what to do in the boardroom when the topic of blockchain emerges is to know what questions to ask and what best practices to put in place now.

The website hackernoon claims that 2018 will be the year blockchain disrupts the technology world forever. Why? It purports that blockchain is the fair and public way to store and transfer information that everyone has wanted since the internet began.

Blockchain has great potential, but also many challenges to overcome. It's exciting to be a part of yet another transformation. As the IBM computer, the internet and Bluetooth showed us in the latter half of the last century, these underlying technologies can take years and even decades to take hold. This time, the entire system of transacting business and determining what has value could be up for grabs.

I think we've shown that most shifts take 10 or more years to fundamentally change our society and business, but each step in the process is important. While this could be a breakthrough year in solving some of the problems that blockchain faces, it will not be the year that blockchain suddenly takes over all of these transactions. It's an overwhelming and daunting concept.

In the next and final chapter, I'll focus in on a checklist and best practices for managing blockchain from the boardroom.

# 5
# BLOCKCHAIN
# IN THE BOARDROOM

I hope this book has provided a good conceptual framework for you to consider the implications of blockchain for your business. Now, let's break it down into practical steps.

Start with getting a handle on how blockchain will affect your business. A good exercise for any company, large or small, is what I refer to as Blockchain Mapping,™ where you gather the key stakeholders in your organization (i.e., marketing, operations, technology, legal) and conduct a workshop to evaluate how your business could be affected by blockchain technology.

While blockchain could be a five- to 10-year or more transformation, the impact is large enough that it's worth investing time to consider the possibilities now and then determine appropriate benchmarks for reevaluation and/or a reasonable roadmap to study this at a deeper level. The key issue is determining the cost and resource allocation, and potential return on investment, over time.

## Blockchain Mapping™

There are two components to blockchain mapping. The first is to evaluate the scope of blockchain uses and determine what functions blockchain performs that *could* have an impact on your business and industry in the future. Go around the map and consider how blockchain technology could disrupt how you handle each of the following areas. You should consider this in two contexts: your relationship with your customers and your relationship with your suppliers. The purpose of this exercise is to evaluate the possible current state of suppliers and customers with the potential future state of blockchain.

- Real estate ownership or rights

- Financial transactions (i.e., borrowing money, lines of credit, letters of credit, processing payment, discounts or other forms of transaction completion)

- Product supply tracking

- Manufacturing tracking

- Internet of Things

- Unique ID, password or verification of identity

- Digital rights — distribution of music, photos, video

- Global, nontraditional currency

- Delivery tracking

*[See image next page]*

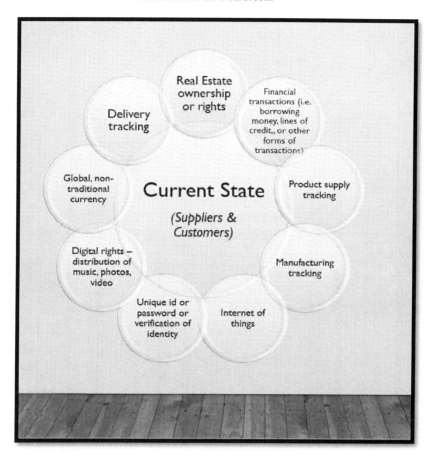

Once you have completed that analysis, layer that map with the considerations noted below. Consider this from two perspectives: your company and your competitors. I recommend conducting an analysis of your competitors in terms of what you know, from a public search, they are doing with blockchain, as well as an analysis of any patents filed by your competitors related to blockchain. This component is intended to help you build on your analysis of potential disruption with the implementation plan that would be required to remain competitive.

What is the time and investment required to implement:

- Replacing legacy systems

- Introducing new products or services

- Accepting new forms of currency

- Using existing blockchain platforms versus building your own

- Connecting the blockchain to the end user

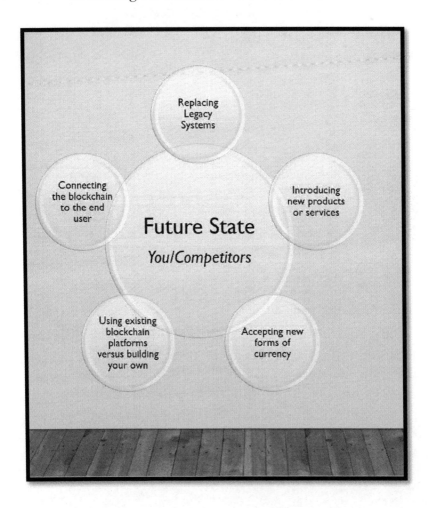

Once you have completed your blockchain mapping analysis and allowed yourself to consider a new set of assumptions, it's time to hold the strategy session to continue with a robust set of questions and discussion that will lead you to important conclusions and best practices for longer-term continued assessment and implementation.

## Questions to Consider

- Does your company use a database that could be replaced by blockchain technology (this should be clear after reading this book)?

- Do you have a team investigating blockchain?

  o Are their goals clearly defined?

  o How will they measure success?

  o Have you given them latitude to think into the future?

- What is the cost to your business if you do nothing?

- Will you use existing platforms? How would you roll out new products or services using blockchain technology? How would you promote that to your customers as an advantage?

- How can you participate in existing blockchain projects?

- How will you track the use of blockchain as an open source solution (in many cases)? In other words, patching blockchain as open source code could become essential to managing the security benefits of the tool and avoid the DAO attack scenario.

- Do you need to track a product through a supply chain?

- Do you currently provide one of the middleman services potentially affected, such as clearing a transaction, providing services related to a transaction, managing digital rights or intellectual property rights of others, enforcing rights, recoding property? If so, what happens when blockchain simply replaces what you do?

- Is it important for your company to be a leader in creating the standards and governance that will form, or would you prefer to simply monitor and follow the leaders?

- Should you be tracking the patents filed by competitors related to this technology to provide guidance on what you should be doing?

- Can you produce software, devices or infrastructure to support blockchain in the future?

- Could you do something to standardize how blockchain gets deployed in devices and the Internet of Things? What additional tools will be needed that you could provide?

- Are you developing IOT, and will you use blockchain in these devices?

- How would you connect blockchain to existing databases?

- What existing databases could later be replaced by blockchain? Should that have an impact on decisions you make about upgrades now? How much time will it take if your legacy systems have to be replaced? How much money? Would you have to run parallel systems and if so, for how long?

- Do you have your own top-level domain operating on the root zone of the internet? If not, should you? There will be another opportunity to acquire one in 2021–2022. If you do, how are you creating a long-range vision that takes into account new technologies being developed, like blockchain?

- Have you considered that blockchain has to operate on top of the internet and whether that should be on an alternative root zone or the existing domain name system?

- Will the connection of things (i.e., a car, refrigerator, device, etc.) with a transaction be important for you?

- How will privacy laws change, and could blockchain help or hurt your ability to comply with those laws across the globe?

- Would your company ever consider accepting new forms of currency? Why or why not? Would your customers want or demand it? If so, how would you transfer that currency into revenue and profits that could be recognized? If so, how does that affect your accounting principles and reporting requirements?

In concluding the session, after asking and answering these and other questions tailored to your business, you can begin to map out a roadmap for a working group to tackle a more-detailed strategic plan and budget for investing in blockchain. The roadmap should include assigning a cross-functional team to research and develop the impact to your organization in more depth with clear goals, objectives and benchmarks for success, as well as mechanisms for reporting back in for further decision making.

It's also a good idea, after arming yourself with this information, to put best practices in place for C-suite executives and the board to remain ahead of the potential disruption that will be caused by blockchain.

## C-Suite Leadership Best Practices

- Blockchain will cross over many facets of the organization. Don't allow this to be a silo project in one lane of the company, like technology often is. Your chief officers — who oversee digital, product development, digital marketing, operations and legal — should all be involved in important decision-making and have someone from their team assigned to the research working group.

- Clearly define and document the company point of view on blockchain and how the company could be affected. The assumptions you can accept may change in the future, so be prepared to revisit this at least twice a year. Communicate this throughout your organization so you eliminate misunderstandings that could have a negative impact on your strategy.

- Push boundaries and question your assumptions at least quarterly. Things will change rapidly.

- Get outside objective advice regularly from different perspectives. Inside people can carry out plans and tasks, and gather information, but ensure you are constantly getting a fresh perspective on the subject to avoid a status quo mentality blinding you from important information. Additionally, as a burgeoning area, you want to get a wide range of advice and perspectives to ensure you don't miss an important line of thought leadership.

- Carefully evaluate how to use the many platforms that are forming and choose wisely. This is not easy to unravel once your start building out products and services on blockchain.

- Expect consolidation in the blockchain solution providers.

- Expect regulation in the future that could affect how you are developing and using blockchain.

- Create R&D teams to investigate and fund them without an immediate need for ROI.

- Consider how crossover areas affect this, such as changes in internet policy, privacy requirements, cybersecurity, regulation, policy and best practices.

- Consider how you will position your company — will you be a fast follower or a leader? Will you get involved in how the standards and governance principles are formed, or simply abide by them once they are developed?

- Do you have opportunities to benefit from the profits to be made? Think about how Oracle, Intel, Microsoft, Verizon, Time Warner and Comcast capitalized on the burgeoning computer industry of the 1980s or internet of the 1990s and early 2000s .

- Consider for a moment who will make money — the company that:

  - Creates the default standard that financial institutions and governments use to transition to a blockchain-based way of doing things.

  - Embeds standards into things.

  - Creates the standardized way for consumers to engage with it.

  - Understands how to communicate this, sell it, lobby for it, gain trust and transform everything.

  - Lobbies for the changes needed for new currencies and/or transaction methods to become accepted.

## Board Oversight Best Practices

In the boardroom, the role of directors is a little different. The key for directors is to be properly and objectively informed, ask important and key questions of senior management, and oversee the potential risk to the company if it fails to assess the coming blockchain revolution properly.

This is very much like going back to 1994 when the internet began. Your role in the board is to ensure that you are not rendered obsolete because management doesn't recognize a major change or moves too slowly in comparison to competitors. Consider these best practices.

- Schedule regular briefings by outside experts — be sure you are getting an objective perspective, particularly if you are in a target industry that will be affected. This could be done in conjunction with regular briefings about new technologies to ensure you are getting a wide range of training and education about technologies that could intersect with blockchain and how it could affect your organization. Ask the tough questions.

- Form a sub-task group to meet more regularly with the senior management overseeing the blockchain team. A sample agenda of this meeting could include:

  o Current blockchain initiative update

  o Report on competitive activities

  o Development of governance or standards that could affect your organization

  o Impact of new currencies and the use of new currencies by competitors

  o Using existing technology via partnerships or licenses versus building your own technology

  o Updates on new assumptions or breakthroughs

At least once a year, the blockchain working group should provide a full update on the mapping exercise and present this to you.

- Attend conferences focused on director-level education. The National Association of Corporate Directors hosts conferences focused on future trends and technology where blockchain and other cutting-edge trends are discussed at a basic and intermediate level.

- More in-depth conferences can be found on *Coin Telegraph* under Events. There is an increasing number of these events, so be sure it is not a "cryptocurrency" conference. These are high-priced and focused on trading these unregulated currencies.

The blockchain trend is in early days. It's not unlike cybersecurity. As soon as you think you have it handled, you have to create a new checklist to address the new threats and issues.

Change will simply be continual — accept this premise. Most likely, by the time I finish writing this book, get it edited and out there, components already will be outdated or evolving beyond what I have written. That's why I'll keep writing and posting information on my blog. Whether you are a C-suite executive or a director trying to understand blockchain, this book is a starting point. You'll have to continue to read, and stay apprised and continually question everything you hear and read.

If you are a technologist and you made it this far, thank you! I also apologize for any gross oversimplifications that may have offended you. Leadership in this new arena will take communication, education and advocacy at a macro high level, as well as in the weeds, getting the work done to create the transformations required for the visionary blockchain technologies to see a new form of reality.

While some may prefer for things to stay the way they are, I think we all know by now that that won't happen. The pace of change is accelerating. Blockchain is not quite at a tipping point, but it's close. If the technologists can solve a couple of problems (and they will), it will then be up to visionary corporate and government leaders to shepherd in the transition to protect individuals, enhance security, remove redundancies and improve trust.

I've included the resources I used in researching and writing the book, as well as additional helpful resources and conferences to consider to learn more on your own. If you are in a position to influence the future, dig in and help shape it, the future needs you.

*In the middle of difficulty lies opportunity.*
—Albert Einstein

# RESOURCES

To make this resources section most helpful, I've categorized the resources I used into areas of interest, so if a specific topic is of greatest interest, you can find items to review and consider in more depth. I've provided URLs to help you locate this information online.

### White Papers & Presentations by Companies

Adledger Blockchain Consortium. https://adledger.org

CBInisghts. "Blockchain Investment Trends in Review." https://www.cbinsights.com/research/report/blockchain-trends-opportunities/

Cognizant. "Demistifying Blockchain." https://www.cognizant.com/whitepapers/demystifying-blockchain-codex2199.pdf

Enterprise Ethereum Alliance. https://entethalliance.org/

Hyperledger Project. https://hyperledger.org

IBM Blockchain Platform in Action. https://www.ibm.com/blockchain/platform

Intel. Intel Technology Securing Enterprise Blockchains Infographic. https://www.intel.com/content/www/us/en/security/securing-enterprise-blockchains-infographic.html

JP Morgan. "Unlocking Economic Advantage with Blockchain: A Guide for Asset Managers." https://www.jpmorgan.com/global/blockchain

KPMG. "Blockchain: Where the board should start."
https://boardleadership.kpmg.us/relevant-topics/articles/2017/04/blockchain-where-the-board-should-start.html

Samsung. "Samsung SDS Nexledger: A Blockchain Platform Solution."
https://www.samsungsds.com/global/en/solutions/off/nexledger/Nexledger.html

### Articles about Cryptocurrency & Crypto Hacks

Aziz. "4 Reasons Why Now is the Best Time for You to Invest in Cryptocurrencies." Master the Crypto.
https://masterthecrypto.com/invest-in-cryptocurrencies

Finley, Klint. "A $50 Million Hack Just Showed that the DAO Was All Too Human." *WIRED*. June 18, 2016.
https://Wired.com/2016/06/50-million-hack-just-showed-dao-human/

Iyengar, Rishi. "More than $70 million stolen in bitcoin hack." CNN Tech. December 8, 2017.
http://money.com/2017/12/07/technology/nicehas-bitcoin-theft-hacking

Kurtenbach, Elaine. "Bitcoin Worth Millions Stolen Days Before US Exchange Opens." *U.S. News & World Report*. December 7, 2017.
https://www.usnews.com

Moffit, Tyler. "Cryptocurrency hacks: Hacking the unhackable." TEISS Cracking Cybersecurity. August 16, 2017.
https://teiss.co.uk/threats/cryptocurrency-hacks-hacking-unhackable-blockchain-secured-accounts/

Roberts, Jeff John. "How Bitcoin Is Stolen: 5 Common Threats." *Fortune*. December 8, 2017.
http://fortune.com/2017/12/08/bitcoin-theft

Wieczner, Jen. "Hacking Cointbase: The Great Bitcoin Bank Robbery." *Fortune*. August 22, 2017. http://fortune.com/201708/22/bitcoin-coinbase-hack/

## Articles About Companies Using Blockchain & General Blockchain Trends

Aitken, Roger. "IBM & Walmart Launching Blockchain Food Safety Alliance in China with Fortune 500s." *Forbes*. December 14, 2017. https://www.forbes.com/sites/rogeraitken/2017/12/14/ibm-walmart-launching-blockchain-food-safety-alliance-in-china-with-forutne-500-jd-com

Anadiotis, George. "How to use blockchain to build a database solutions." *ZD Net*. March 2, 2017. http://www.zdnet.com/article/blockchains-in-the-database-world-what-for-and-how/

Baumgartner, Jeff. "Comcast Looking to Link Blockchain to the Connected Home." *Multichannel News*. February 9, 2018. http://www.multichannel.com/news/cable-operators/comcast-looking-link-blockchain-connected-home

Berkeley, Jon. "The promise of the blockchain: the trust machine." *The Economist*. October 31, 2015. https://www.economist.com/news/leaders/21677198-technology-behind-bitcoin-could-transofrm-how-economy-works-trust0machine

Bloomberg, Jason. "Eight Reasons To Be Skeptical About Blockchain." *Forbes*. May 31, 2017. https://www.forbest.com/sites/jasonbloomberg/2017/05/31/eight-reasons-to-be-skeptical-about-blockchain

Bloomberg. "Bitcoin Has a Dirty, Dirty Secret." *Fortune*. December 15, 2017. http://fortune.com/2017/12/15/bitcoin-dirty-secret-energy-use-pollution

Cheng, Evelyn, Tausche, Kayla. "Jamie Dimon says if you're

stupid enough to buy bitcoin, you'll pay the price one day." CNBC. October 13, 2017. https://www.cnbc.com/2017/10/13/ka,mie-dimon-says-people-who-buy-bitcoin-are-stupid

Cole, Nicolas. "2018 Will Be the Year Blockchain Technology Goes Mainstream. Here's Why." Hackernoon. January 2, 2018. https://hackernoon.com/2018-will-be-the-year-blockchain-technology-goes-mainstream-heres-why

Corner, Lucrezia. "Media's role in blockchain and crypto, interview with TechCrunch's Mike Butcher." *Coin Telegraph*. January 31, 2018. https://cointelegraph.com/new/medias-role-in-blockchain-and-crypto-interview-with-techcrunchs-mike-butcher

Frank, Jacqui, Chin, Kara, Cadigan, Trevor. "This is one of the best responses to Jamie Dimon calling bitcoin a fraud that we have heard so far." *Business Insider*. December 1, 2017. http://www.businesindier.com/best-response-to-jamie-dimon-calling-bitcoin-a-fraud-2017

Harris, Pete. "Analysis: IT Heavyweights Are Waking Up to Blockchain." *Distributed Ledger*. May, 2017. https://distributed.com/news/analysis-it-heavyweights-are-waking-blockchain

Higgins, Stan. "AQXA Is Using Thereum's Blockchain for a New Flight Insurance Product." *Coin Desk*. September 13, 2017. https://www.coindesk.com/axa-using-ethereums-blockchain-new-flight-insurance-product

Iansiti, Marco, Lakhani, Karim. "The Truth About Blockchain." *Harvard Business Review*. January/Feburary 2017 Issue.

MarArlen, Gary. "Blockchain Technology Moving Into Cable, Advertising Sectors." *Multichannel News*. October 24, 2017. http://www.multichannel.com/blog/i-was-saying/blockchain-technology-moving-cable-advertising-sectors

Nash, Kim. "Blockchain: Catalyst for Massive Change Across

Industries." *Wall Street Journal/CIO Journal*. February 2, 2016. https://blogs.wsj.com/cio/2016/02/02/blockchain-catalyst-for-massive-changes-across-industries

Nash, Kim. "Business Interest in Blockchain Picks Up While Cryptocurrency Causes Conniptions." *Wall Street Journal/CIO Journal*. February 6, 2018. https://blogs.wsj.com/cio/2018/02/06/business-interest-in-blockchain-picks-up-while-cryptocurrency-causes-conniptions

Norton, Steven. "CIO Explainer: What is Blockchain?" *Wall Street Journal/CIO Journal*. February 2, 2016. https://blogs.wsj.com/cio/2016/02/02/cio-explainer-what-is-blockchain

Quora. "What's Stopping Blockchain from Going Mainstream?" Inc. September 21, 2017. https://www.inc.com/quora/whats-stopping-blcockahin-from-going-mainstream

Russell, Jon. "Mark Zuckerberg is right to explore the potential of blockchain for Facebook." *Tech Crunch*. January 5, 2018. https://techcrunch.com/20158/01/05/mark-zuckerberg-is-right-to-explore-the-potential-of-the-blockchain-for-facebook

## Articles About Blockchain & the Domain Name System

Garcia, Aiai. "How the Blockchain Could Have Prevent the DNS Denial of Service Attack." *Consensys*. October 21, 2016. https://media.consensys.net/how-the-blockchain-could-have-prevent-the-dns-denial-of-service-attack

Johnson, Nick. "Hosting a DNS domain on the blockchain." Hackernoon. January 4, 2017. https://hackernoon.com/hosting-a-dns-domain-on-th-blockchain

Ward, Mike. "Change is Coming: How the Blockchain Will Transform the Domain Name Business." *Cointelegraph*. April 23, 2015. https://cointelegraph.com/news/change-is-coming-how-the-blockchain-will-transform-the-domain-name-business


## Initial Coin Offerings & the Stock Impact

Clayton, Jay, SEC Chairman. "Statement on Cryptocurrencies and Initial Coin Offerings." SEC Public Statement. December 11, 2017. https://sec.gov/news/public-statement/statement-clayton-2017-12-11

Roose, Kevin. "Kodak's Dubious Cryptocurrency Gamble." *New York Times*. January 30, 2018. https://nytimes.com/2018/01/30/technology/kodak-blockchain-bitcoin.html

Shapira, Arie and Leinz, Kaley. "Long Island Iced Tea Soars After Changing Its Name to Long Blockchain." Bloomberg. December 21, 2017. https://www.bloomberg.com/news/articles/2017/12/21/crypto-craze-sees-long-island-iced-tea-rename-as-long-blockchain


## Articles about Blockchain Start-up & Emerging Companies

AWS Case Study: Coinbase. https://aws.amazon.com/solutions/case-studies/coinbase

Masters, Blythe. "The revolution beyond bitcoin. Blockchain technology will spread fast in finance." *The Economist – The World in 2018*. http://www.theworldin.com/article/10635/edition2016revolution-beyond-bitcoin

Russo, Camilla. "Goldman and Google Are Among the Most Active Blockchain Investors." Bloomberg. October 17, 2017. https://www.bloomberg.com/news/articles/2017/-10-17/goldman-google-make-list-of-most-active-blockchain-investors

Stark, Harold. "Keep An Eye on These Blockchain Start-ups Throughout 2018." *Forbes*. December 12, 107. https://www.forbest.com/sites/haroldstark/2017/12/12/keep-an-eye-on-these-blockchain-start-ups-throughout-2018/2

## Historical References

Johnston, Robyn. "5 of the oldest U.S. Tech Companies – and their unusual histories." *Venture Beat*. February 27, 2014. https://2014/02/27/5-of-the-oldest-u-s-tech-companies-an-their-unusual-histories

History of IBM. https://www-03.ibm.com/ibm/history/history/history_intro.html

History of Oracle. http://oracle.com.edgesuite.net/timeline/oracle/

History of Verizon Communications. https://www.verizon.com/about/sites/default/files/Verizon_Corporate_History.pdf

Fortune, Steve. "A Brief History of Databases." Avant.Org Project. February 27, 2014. http://avant.org/project/history-of-databases/

Larson, Matt. ICANN DNS Primer, GDD Industry Summit presented May 11, 2017. Slideshare.net/ICANNpresentations

National Academic Press (https://www.nap.edu/read/11258/chapter/4

Newberger, Eric C., "Home Computers and Internet Use in the United States: August 2000," *Current Population Reports*, U.S. Department of Commerce, U.S. Census Bureau, Washington, DC, September 2001, available at http://www.census.gov/prod/2001pubs/p23-207.pdf

Nordic Semicondcutor. "A short history of Bluetooth." July 14, 2014. https://www.nordicsemi.com/eng/News/ULP-Wireless-Update/A-short-history-of-Bluetooth

Pothitos, Adam. "The History of Bluetooth." August 2, 2017 *Mobile Industry Review.* http://www.mboileindustryreview.com/2017/08/the-history-of-bluethooth

Statement of Policy on Management of Internet Names and Addresses. https://www.ntia.doc.gov/federal-register-notice/1998/statement-policy-management-internet-names-and-addresses

## Books

Antonopoulos, Andreas. *The Internet of Money.* Merkle Bloom LLC, 2016.

Cody, Isaac. *Blockchain Technology: Innovative and modern financial framework that will revolutionize the next digital economy with blockchain technology.* 2017.

Diedrich, Henning. *Ethereum: blockchains, digital assets, smart contracts, decentralized autonomous organizations.* Wildfire Publishing. 2016.

Mougayar, William. *The Business Blockchain: promise, practice, and application of the next Internet technology.* Wiley. 2016.

Swan, Melanie. *Blockchain: Blueprint for a new economy.* O'Reilly. 2015.

Tapscott, Don, Tapscott, Alex. *Blockchain Revolution: how the technology behind bitcoin is changing money, business, and the world.* Penguin. 2016.

## Patents Referenced

See table on following pages.

# US Blockchain Patents through February 2018

| Serial/Reg Number | Title | Patent Owner |
|---|---|---|
| 20170279818 | ANTIVIRUS SIGNATURE DISTRIBUTION WITH DISTRIBUTED LEDGER | ACCENTURE GLOBAL SOLUTIONS LIMITED; |
| 20170279783 | SECURE 3D MODEL SHARING USING DISTRIBUTED LEDGER | ACCENTURE GLOBAL SOLUTIONS LIMITED; |
| 20170054611 | TRUST FRAMEWORK FOR PLATFORM DATA | ACCENTURE GLOBAL SOLUTIONS LIMITED; |
| 20170206522 | DEVICE, METHOD AND SYSTEM FOR AUTONOMOUS SELECTION OF A COMMODITY SUPPLIER THROUGH A BLOCKCHAIN DISTRIBUTED DATABASE | ACCENTURE GLOBAL SOLUTIONS LIMITED; |
| 20170338947 | REWRITABLE BLOCKCHAIN | ACCENTURE GLOBAL SOLUTIONS LIMITED;GSC SECRYPT, LLC; |
| 20170338957 | REWRITABLE BLOCKCHAIN | ACCENTURE GLOBAL SOLUTIONS LIMITED;GSC SECRYPT, LLC; |
| 9785369 | Multiple-link blockchain | ACCENTURE GLOBAL SOLUTIONS LIMITED;GSC Secrypt, LLC; |
| 9774578 | Distributed key secret for rewritable blockchain | ACCENTURE GLOBAL SOLUTIONS LIMITED;GSC Secrypt, LLC; |
| '20180032273' | "HYBRID BLOCKCHAIN" | ACCENTURE GLOBAL SOLUTIONS LIMITED;GSC Secrypt, LLC; |
| '20180048469' | "WRAPPED-UP BLOCKCHAIN" | ACCENTURE GLOBAL SOLUTIONS LIMITED;GSC Secrypt, LLC; |
| 20170374049 | DISTRIBUTED KEY SECRET FOR REWRITABLE BLOCKCHAIN | Accenture Global Solutions;GSC Secrypt; |
| 20170331635 | SYSTEM AND METHOD FOR FILE TIME-STAMPING USING A BLOCKCHAIN NETWORK | ACRONIS |
| 20170364655 | MONITORING ADHERENCE TO A HEALTHCARE PLAN | AFTECHMOBILE INC. (D/B/A MOBRISE INC.); |
| 20170324738 | INTERNET SECURITY | ALCATEL-LUCENT USA INC.; |
| 7203842 | Method and apparatus for secure configuration of a field programmable gate array | ALGOTRONIX, LTD.; |
| 20170364698 | FRAGMENTING DATA FOR THE PURPOSES OF PERSISTENT STORAGE ACROSS MULTIPLE IMMUTABLE DATA STRUCTURES | ALTR SOLUTIONS, INC.; |
| 20170364701 | STORING DIFFERENTIALS OF FILES IN A DISTRIBUTED BLOCKCHAIN | ALTR SOLUTIONS, INC.; |
| 20170366353 | GENERATION OF HASH VALUES WITHIN A BLOCKCHAIN | ALTR SOLUTIONS, INC.; |
| 20170364700 | IMMUTABLE LOGGING OF ACCESS REQUESTS TO DISTRIBUTED FILE SYSTEMS | ALTR SOLUTIONS, INC.; |
| 9703986 | Decentralized reputation service for synthetic identities | Anonyome Labs, Inc.; |
| 20170353320 | OBTAINING AND USING TIME INFORMATION ON A SECURE ELEMENT (SE) | APPLE INC.; |
| RE39994 | Polyetheresteramides and compositions of antistatic polymers containing the same | ARKEMA;ARKEMA FRANCE; |
| 8299138 | Process for producing flexible polyurethane foam | ASAHI GLASS COMPANY, LIMITED; |
| 6815467 | Methods for producing a polyol and a polymer dispersed polyol | ASAHI GLASS COMPANY, LIMITED; |
| 6759448 | Flexible polyurethane foam, its production method and material system for its production | ASAHI GLASS COMPANY, LIMITED; |

# US Blockchain Patents through February 2018

| Serial/Reg Number | Title | Patent Owner |
|---|---|---|
| 8143343 | Microphase-separated structure, immobilized microphase-separated structure and wavelength-variable laser oscillator, temperature sensor and light filter using the structure | ASAHI KASEI EMD CORPORATION;HAMAMATSU PHOTONICS K.K.;JAPAN AEROSPACE EXPLORATION AGENCY;NATIONAL UNIVERSITY CORPORATION NAGOYA INSTITUTE OF TECHNOLOGY; |
| 20170029614 | Thermoplastic Elastomer Composition, Stopper for Medical Container, and Medical Container | ASAHI KASEI KABUSHIKI KAISHA; |
| 6706851 | Polyetheresteramides and compositions of antistatic polymers containing the same | ATOFINA; |
| 20170295157 | SMARTPHONE FRAUD-PROOF AUTHORIZATION AND AUTHENTICATION FOR SECURE INTERACTIONS | AVAYA INC.; |
| 20170364552 | Ensuring Data Integrity of Executed Transactions | Bank New York Mellon |
| 20170366516 | MANAGING VERIFIABLE, CRYPTOGRAPHICALLY STRONG TRANSACTIONS | Bank New York Mellon |
| 20170366357 | DISTRIBUTED, CENTRALLY AUTHORED BLOCK CHAIN NETWORK | Bank New York Mellon |
| 20170243177 | SYSTEM FOR ROUTING OF PROCESS AUTHORIZATION AND SETTLEMENT TO A USER IN PROCESS DATA NETWORK BASED ON SPECIFIED PARAMETERS | BANK OF AMERICA CORPORATION; |
| 20170243208 | SYSTEM FOR CONTROL OF DEVICE IDENTITY AND USAGE IN A PROCESS DATA NETWORK | BANK OF AMERICA CORPORATION; |
| 20170243212 | SYSTEM FOR IMPLEMENTING A DISTRIBUTED LEDGER ACROSS MULTIPLE NETWORK NODES | BANK OF AMERICA CORPORATION; |
| 20170243213 | SYSTEM TO ENABLE CONTACTLESS ACCESS TO A TRANSACTION TERMINAL USING A PROCESS DATA NETWORK | BANK OF AMERICA CORPORATION; |
| 20170243214 | SYSTEM FOR TRACKING TRANSFER OF RESOURCES IN A PROCESS DATA NETWORK | BANK OF AMERICA CORPORATION; |
| 20170243215 | SYSTEM FOR EXTERNAL SECURE ACCESS TO PROCESS DATA NETWORK | BANK OF AMERICA CORPORATION; |
| 20170243217 | SYSTEM FOR ROUTING OF PROCESS AUTHORIZATIONS AND SETTLEMENT TO A USER IN A PROCESS DATA NETWORK | BANK OF AMERICA CORPORATION; |
| 20170243222 | SYSTEM FOR USE OF SECURE DATA FROM A PROCESS DATA NETWORK AS SECURED ACCESS BY USERS | BANK OF AMERICA CORPORATION; |
| 20170243286 | SYSTEM FOR ALLOWING EXTERNAL VALIDATION OF DATA IN A PROCESS DATA NETWORK | BANK OF AMERICA CORPORATION; |
| 20170243287 | SYSTEM FOR MANAGING SERIALIZABILITY OF RESOURCE TRANSFERS IN A PROCESS DATA NETWORK | BANK OF AMERICA CORPORATION; |
| 20170244707 | SYSTEM FOR ESTABLISHING SECURE ACCESS FOR USERS IN A PROCESS DATA NETWORK | BANK OF AMERICA CORPORATION; |
| 20170244721 | SYSTEM FOR PROVIDING LEVELS OF SECURITY ACCESS TO A PROCESS DATA NETWORK | BANK OF AMERICA CORPORATION; |
| 20170243025 | SYSTEM FOR EXTERNAL VALIDATION OF DISTRIBUTED RESOURCE STATUS | BANK OF AMERICA CORPORATION; |
| 20170244720 | SYSTEM FOR EXTERNAL VALIDATION OF PRIVATE-TO-PUBLIC TRANSITION PROTOCOLS | BANK OF AMERICA CORPORATION; |
| 20170244757 | SYSTEM FOR EXTERNAL VALIDATION OF SECURE PROCESS TRANSACTIONS | BANK OF AMERICA CORPORATION; |
| 20170243209 | SYSTEM FOR GRANT OF USER ACCESS AND DATA USAGE IN A PROCESS DATA NETWORK | BANK OF AMERICA CORPORATION; |
| 20170279800 | ENHANCING AUTHENTICATION AND SOURCE OF PROOF THROUGH A DYNAMICALLY UPDATABLE BIOMETRICS DATABASE | BANK OF AMERICA CORPORATION; |
| 20170295232 | SYSTEM FOR TRANSFORMING LARGE SCALE ELECTRONIC PROCESSING USING APPLICATION BLOCK CHAIN | BANK OF AMERICA CORPORATION; |

# US Blockchain Patents through February 2018

| Serial/Reg Number | Title | Patent Owner |
|---|---|---|
| 20170076286 | CONTROLLING ACCESS TO DATA | BANK OF AMERICA CORPORATION; |
| 20170214699 | SYSTEM FOR CONVERSION OF AN INSTRUMENT FROM A NON-SECURED INSTRUMENT TO A SECURED INSTRUMENT IN A PROCESS DATA NETWORK | BANK OF AMERICA CORPORATION; |
| 20170331810 | SYSTEM FOR MANAGING SECURITY AND ACCESS TO RESOURCE SUB-COMPONENTS | BANK OF AMERICA CORPORATION; |
| 20170132630 | BLOCK CHAIN ALIAS FOR PERSON-TO-PERSON PAYMENTS | BANK OF AMERICA CORPORATION; |
| 20170132615 | BLOCK CHAIN ALIAS FOR PERSON-TO-PERSON PAYMENTS | BANK OF AMERICA CORPORATION; |
| 20150363777 | CRYPTOCURRENCY SUSPICIOUS USER ALERT SYSTEM | BANK OF AMERICA CORPORATION; |
| 20170330159 | RESOURCE ALLOCATION AND TRANSFER IN A DISTRIBUTED NETWORK | BANK OF AMERICA CORPORATION; |
| 20170293503 | SYSTEM FOR TRANSFORMING LARGE SCALE ELECTRONIC PROCESSING USING APPLICATION BLOCK CHAIN AND MULTI-STRUCTURED DATA STORES | BANK OF AMERICA CORPORATION; |
| 20170228734 | SYSTEM FOR SECURE ROUTING OF DATA TO VARIOUS NETWORKS FROM A PROCESS DATA NETWORK | BANK OF AMERICA CORPORATION; |
| 20170230353 | SYSTEM FOR CONTROL OF SECURE ACCESS AND COMMUNICATION WITH DIFFERENT PROCESS DATA NETWORKS WITH SEPARATE SECURITY FEATURES | BANK OF AMERICA CORPORATION; |
| 20170230375 | SYSTEM FOR CENTRALIZED CONTROL OF SECURE ACCESS TO PROCESS DATA NETWORK | BANK OF AMERICA CORPORATION; |
| 20170213221 | SYSTEM FOR TRACKING AND VALIDATION OF MULTIPLE INSTANCES OF AN ENTITY IN A PROCESS DATA NETWORK | BANK OF AMERICA CORPORATION; |
| 9825931 | System for tracking and validation of an entity in a process data network | BANK OF AMERICA CORPORATION; |
| 20150363783 | CRYPTOCURRENCY RISK DETECTION SYSTEM | BANK OF AMERICA CORPORATION; |
| 20170140408 | TRANSPARENT SELF-MANAGING REWARDS PROGRAM USING BLOCKCHAIN AND SMART CONTRACTS | BANK OF AMERICA CORPORATION; |
| 20160203572 | METHOD TO SECURELY ESTABLISH, AFFIRM, AND TRANSFER OWNERSHIP OF ARTWORKS | BIGCHAINDB GMBH; |
| 20160300234 | SYSTEM AND METHOD FOR DECENTRALIZED TITLE RECORDATION AND AUTHENTICATION | bitmark |
| 20160283941 | SYSTEMS AND METHODS FOR PERSONAL IDENTIFICATION AND VERIFICATION | BLACK GOLD COIN, INC.; |
| 20170206382 | CRYPTOGRAPHIC ASIC INCLUDING CIRCUITRY-ENCODED TRANSFORMATION FUNCTION | BLOCKCHAIN ASICS LLC; |
| 9608829 | System and method for creating a multi-branched blockchain with configurable protocol rules | BLOCKCHAIN TECHNOLOGIES CORPORATION; |
| 20170352219 | SYSTEM AND METHOD FOR SECURELY RECEIVING AND COUNTING VOTES IN AN ELECTION | Blockchain Technologies Corporation; |
| 9836908 | System and method for securely receiving and counting votes in an election | Blockchain Technologies Corporation; |
| 20170236123 | DECENTRALIZED PROCESSING OF GLOBAL NAMING SYSTEMS | BLOCKSTACK INC.; |
| 20160358165 | CRYPTOGRAPHICALLY CONCEALING AMOUNTS TRANSACTED ON A LEDGER WHILE PRESERVING A NETWORK'S ABILITY TO VERIFY THE TRANSACTION | BLOCKSTREAM |
| 9807106 | Mitigating blockchain attack | BRITISH TELECOMMUNICATIONS PUBLIC LIMITED COMPANY; |

# US Blockchain Patents through February 2018

| Serial/Reg Number | Title | Patent Owner |
|---|---|---|
| 20170344983 | BIXCoin: A Secure Peer-to-Peer Payment System Based on the Public Payments Ledger | BUSINESS INFORMATION EXCHANGE SYSTEM CORP.; |
| 9635000 | Blockchain identity management system based on public identities ledger | BUSINESS INFORMATION EXCHANGE SYSTEM CORP.; |
| '20180054491' | "MAINTAINING DISTRIBUTED STATE AMONG STATELESS SERVICE CLIENTS" | CA, INC.; |
| 20170221029 | BLOCKCHAINING SYSTEMS AND METHODS FOR FRICTIONLESS MEDIA | CABLE TELEVISION LABORATORIES, INC.; |
| 20170134161 | BLOCKCHAINING FOR MEDIA DISTRIBUTION | CABLE TELEVISION LABORATORIES, INC.; |
| 20170337534 | SYSTEMS AND METHODS FOR BLOCKCHAIN VIRTUALIZATION AND SCALABILITY | CABLE TELEVISION LABORATORIES, INC.; |
| 20170206523 | SYSTEMS AND METHODS FOR DIGITAL ASSET SECURITY ECOSYSTEMS | CABLE TELEVISION LABORATORIES, INC.; |
| 9749140 | Systems and methods for managing digital identities | Cambridge Blockchain, LLC; |
| 9667427 | Systems and methods for managing digital identities | Cambridge Blockchain, LLC; |
| 20170366348 | BLOCKCHAIN SYSTEMS AND METHODS FOR USER AUTHENTICATION | CAPITAL ONE SERVICES, LLC; |
| 20170358041 | SYSTEMS AND METHODS FOR ADVANCED ENERGY SETTLEMENTS, NETWORK-BASED MESSAGING, AND APPLICATIONS SUPPORTING THE SAME ON A BLOCKCHAIN PLATFORM | CAUSAM ENERGY, INC.; |
| 9338148 | Secure distributed information and password management | CELLCO PARTNERSHIP D/B/A VERIZON WIRELESS;VERIZON PATENT AND LICENSING INC.; |
| 20130274422 | POLYCARBONATES AS NUCLEATING AGENTS FOR POLYLACTIDES | CENTRE NATIONAL DE LA RECHERCHE SCIENTIFIQUE;TOTAL RESEARCH & TECHNOLOGY FELUY; |
| 20170103458 | Derivative Contracts that Settle Based on a Virtual Currency Difficulty Factor or an Index of Virtual Currency Generation Yield | CHICAGO MERCANTILE EXCHANGE INC.; |
| '20180039667' | "SYSTEMS AND METHODS FOR BLOCKCHAIN RULE SYNCHRONIZATION" | CHICAGO MERCANTILE EXCHANGE INC.; |
| '20180032759' | "OPEN REGISTRY FOR HUMAN IDENTIFICATION" | CHRONICLED INC |
| 20170345019 | OPEN REGISTRY FOR INTERNET OF THINGS | CHRONICLED, INC.; |
| 20160358186 | OPEN REGISTRY FOR IDENTITY OF THINGS | CHRONICLED, INC.; |
| 20170302663 | BLOCK CHAIN BASED IoT DEVICE IDENTITY VERIFICATION AND ANOMALY DETECTION | CISCO TECHNOLOGY, INC.; |
| 9871775 | Group membership block chain | CISCO TECHNOLOGY, INC.; |
| 5491815 | Method and device for controlling timers associated with multiple users in a data processing system | CISCO TECHNOLOGY, INC.; |
| 20170317833 | METHODS AND APPARATUS FOR PROVIDING ATTESTATION OF INFORMATION USING A CENTRALIZED OR DISTRIBUTED LEDGER | civic technologies |
| 20170317834 | METHODS AND SYSTEMS OF PROVIDING VERIFICATION OF INFORMATION USING A CENTRALIZED OR DISTRIBUTED LEDGER | civic technologies |
| 20170287090 | SYSTEM AND METHOD FOR CREATING AND EXECUTING DATA-DRIVEN LEGAL CONTRACTS | CLAUSE, INC.; |
| 9436935 | Computer system for making a payment using a tip button | Coinbase, Inc.; |
| 20150262137 | OFF-BLOCK CHAIN TRANSACTIONS IN COMBINATION WITH ON-BLOCK CHAIN TRANSACTIONS | Coinbase, Inc.; |
| 20170308872 | DIGITAL VIRTUAL CURRENCY TRANSACTION SYSTEM AND METHOD HAVING BLOCK CHAIN BETWEEN CONCERNED PARTIES | COINPLUG, INC.; |

# US Blockchain Patents through February 2018

| Serial/Reg Number | Title | Patent Owner |
|---|---|---|
| 20170330179 | METHOD FOR ISSUING AUTHENTICATION INFORMATION AND BLOCKCHAIN-BASED SERVER USING THE SAME | COINPLUG, INC.; |
| 20170330180 | METHOD FOR USING AND REVOKING AUTHENTICATION INFORMATION AND BLOCKCHAIN-BASED SERVER USING THE SAME | COINPLUG, INC.; |
| 20170316497 | METHOD FOR CREATING, REGISTERING, REVOKING AUTHENTICATION INFORMATION AND SERVER USING THE SAME | COINPLUG, INC.; |
| 20170322992 | Distributed Data Access Control | COMCAST CABLE COMMUNICATIONS, LLC; |
| 20170352027 | AUTHENTICATED DATA FEED FOR BLOCKCHAINS | Cornell University |
| 20170364936 | COMPUTER-IMPLEMENTED ELECTRONIC COUPON SYSTEM AND METHODS USING A BLOCKCHAIN | CouponCo Ltd.; |
| 9747586 | System and method for issuance of electronic currency substantiated by a reserve of assets | CPN GOLD B.V. |
| 20170372278 | PAYMENT SYSTEM FOR CARRYING OUT ELECTRONIC SETTLEMENTS USING BLOCKCHAIN TECHNOLOGY | CPN GOLD B.V. PLLC; |
| 20160267605 | SYSTEM AND METHOD FOR ESTABLISHING A PUBLIC LEDGER FOR GIFT CARD TRANSACTIONS | CREDIT SUISSE, CAYMAN ISLANDS BRANCH; |
| 20160335628 | SYSTEM AND METHOD FOR DIGITAL CURRENCY STORAGE, PAYMENT AND CREDIT | CRYPTYK INC; |
| 6199121 | High speed dynamic chaining of DMA operations without suspending a DMA controller or incurring race conditions | CSR TECHNOLOGY INC.;OAK TECHNOLOGY, INC.; |
| 20170236102 | Peer-to-Peer Financial Transactions Using A Private Distributed Ledger | D+H USA CORPORATION; |
| 20170236103 | Peer-to-Peer Financial Transactions Using A Private Distributed Ledger | D+H USA CORPORATION; |
| 20170236104 | Peer-to-Peer Financial Transactions Using A Private Distributed Ledger | D+H USA CORPORATION; |
| 20160300222 | OFF NETWORK IDENTITY TRACKING IN ANONYMOUS CRYPTOCURRENCY EXCHANGE NETWORKS | datient inc |
| 20160335533 | System and Method for an Autonomous Entity | DAVIS, JOSHUA PAUL; |
| 20170331896 | METHODS AND SYSTEMS FOR PROCESSING ASSETS | DE LA RUE INTERNATIONAL LIMITED; |
| 20170031676 | BLOCKCHAIN COMPUTER DATA DISTRIBUTION | DEJA VU SECURITY, LLC; |
| 20160261404 | METHODS AND SYSTEMS FOR OBFUSCATING DATA AND COMPUTATIONS DEFINED IN A SECURE DISTRIBUTED TRANSACTION LEDGER | DELL PRODUCTS L.P.; |
| 20160260171 | SYSTEMS AND METHODS FOR A COMMODITY CONTRACTS MARKET USING A SECURE DISTRIBUTED TRANSACTION LEDGER | DELL PRODUCTS L.P.; |
| 20160260095 | Containerized Computational Task Execution Management Using a Secure Distributed Transaction Ledger | DELL PRODUCTS L.P.; |
| 20170180469 | METHOD AND SYSTEM FOR FORMING COMPUTE CLUSTERS USING BLOCK CHAINS | DELL PRODUCTS L.P.; |
| 20160259937 | DEVICE REPORTING AND PROTECTION SYSTEMS AND METHODS USING A SECURE DISTRIBUTED TRANSACTIONAL LEDGER | DELL PRODUCTS L.P.; |
| 20160261685 | DEFERRED CONFIGURATION OR INSTRUCTION EXECUTION USING A SECURE DISTRIBUTED TRANSACTION LEDGER | DELL PRODUCTS L.P.; |
| 20160261690 | COMPUTING DEVICE CONFIGURATION AND MANAGEMENT USING A SECURE DECENTRALIZED TRANSACTION LEDGER | DELL PRODUCTS L.P.; |
| 20160299918 | Device Control Using a Secure Decentralized Transactional Ledger | DELL SOFTWARE INC.; |
| 20160292680 | DIGITAL ASSET INTERMEDIARY ELECTRONIC SETTLEMENT PLATFORM | DIGITAL ASSET HOLDINGS; |
| 20170316391 | DIGITAL ASSET MODELING | DIGITAL ASSET HOLDINGS; |

# US Blockchain Patents through February 2018

| Serial/Reg Number | Title | Patent Owner |
|---|---|---|
| 20170308893 | ASSET AND OBLIGATION MANAGEMENT USING FLEXIBLE SETTLEMENT TIMES | DIGITAL ASSET HOLDINGS; |
| 20170103385 | DIGITAL ASSET INTERMEDIARY ELECTRONIC SETTLEMENT PLATFORM | DIGITAL ASSET HOLDINGS; |
| 20170103390 | DIGITAL ASSET INTERMEDIARY ELECTRONIC SETTLEMENT PLATFORM | DIGITAL ASSET HOLDINGS; |
| 20170103391 | DIGITAL ASSET INTERMEDIARY ELECTRONIC SETTLEMENT PLATFORM | DIGITAL ASSET HOLDINGS; |
| 20160358135 | DIGITAL CURRENCY MANAGEMENT METHOD AND DIGITAL CURRENCY NODE APPARATUS | DIQI, INC;WIFIRE OPEN NETWORK GROUP LIMITED; |
| 20160358253 | ELECTRONIC CURRENCY MANAGEMENT METHOD AND ELECTRONIC CURRENCY SYSTEM | DIQI, INC;WIFIRE OPEN NETWORK GROUP LIMITED; |
| 20170228822 | BLOCKCHAIN TECHNOLOGY TO SETTLE TRANSACTIONS | domus tower |
| '20180041571' | "DISTRIBUTED DATA STORE FOR MANAGING MEDIA" | Dot Blockchain Music, Inc. |
| '20180039942' | "DISTRIBUTED DATA STORE FOR MANAGING MEDIA" | Dot Blockchain Music, Inc. |
| 20170185998 | METHOD AND DEVICE FOR PROTECTING ACCESS TO WALLETS IN WHICH CRYPTO CURRENCIES ARE STORED | draglet gmbh |
| 20170178237 | COMPUTER IMPLEMENTED FRAMEWORKS AND METHODS CONFIGURED TO CREATE AND MANAGE A VIRTUAL CURRENCY | DRAGONFLY FINTECH PTE LTD |
| '20180040007' | "TRUSTED PLATFORM AND INTEGRATED BOP APPLICATIONS FOR NETWORKING BOP COMPONENTS" | DUN & BRADSTREET, INC.; |
| 20170161439 | RECORDS ACCESS AND MANAGEMENT | EINGOT LLC; |
| 20150244690 | GENERALIZED ENTITY NETWORK TRANSLATION (GENT) | ENT Technologies, Inc.; |
| 8623976 | Polymerization catalyst compositions containing metallocene complexes and polymers produced by using the same | epislon |
| 20170243241 | Methods and Systems for Regulating Operation of Units Using Encryption Techniques Associated with a Blockchain | Fidelity |
| 20160098730 | System and Method for Block-Chain Verification of Goods | filing cabinet |
| 20160162897 | System and method for user authentication using crypto-currency transactions as access tokens | filing cabinet |
| 20170279801 | SYSTEMS AND METHODS FOR PROVIDING BLOCK CHAIN-BASED MULTIFACTOR PERSONAL IDENTITY VERIFICATION | FINTECH FUND FAMILY LIMITED PARTNERSHIP; |
| 20170221052 | Computationally Efficient Transfer Processing and Auditing Apparatuses, Methods and Systems | FMR LLC; |
| 20170048209 | Crypto Key Recovery and Social Aggregating, Fractionally Efficient Transfer Guidance, Conditional Triggered Transaction, Datastructures, Apparatuses, Methods and Systems | FMR LLC; |
| 20170048235 | Crypto Captcha and Social Aggregating, Fractionally Efficient Transfer Guidance, Conditional Triggered Transaction, Datastructures, Apparatuses, Methods and Systems | FMR LLC; |
| 20170046689 | Crypto Voting and Social Aggregating, Fractionally Efficient Transfer Guidance, Conditional Triggered Transaction, Datastructures, Apparatuses, Methods and Systems | FMR LLC; |
| 20170228731 | Computationally Efficient Transfer Processing and Auditing Apparatuses, Methods and Systems | FMR LLC; |
| 20170109735 | Computationally Efficient Transfer Processing and Auditing Apparatuses, Methods and Systems | FMR LLC; |
| 20170091756 | Point-to-Point Transaction Guidance Apparatuses, Methods and Systems | FMR LLC; |

| Serial/Reg Number | Title | Patent Owner |
|---|---|---|
| 20170083907 | Point-to-Point Transaction Guidance Apparatuses, Methods and Systems | FMR LLC; |
| 20170085555 | Point-to-Point Transaction Guidance Apparatuses, Methods and Systems | FMR LLC; |
| 20170017954 | Point-to-Point Transaction Guidance Apparatuses, Methods and Systems | FMR LLC; |
| 20170017936 | Point-to-Point Transaction Guidance Apparatuses, Methods and Systems | FMR LLC; |
| 20170017955 | Point-to-Point Transaction Guidance Apparatuses, Methods and Systems | FMR LLC; |
| 20170085545 | Smart Rules and Social Aggregating, Fractionally Efficient Transfer Guidance, Conditional Triggered Transaction, Datastructures, Apparatuses, Methods and Systems | FMR LLC; |
| 20170255950 | SYSTEMS AND METHODS FOR PROVIDING BLOCK CHAIN STATE PROOFS FOR PREDICTION MARKET RESOLUTION | FORECAST FOUNDATION OU; |
| 20170249482 | INFORMATION PROCESSING APPARATUS AND NON-TRANSITORY COMPUTER READABLE MEDIUM | FUJI XEROX CO., LTD.; |
| 20170243284 | SECURE PLATFORM AND DATA REPOSITORY FOR FUR OR SKIN COMMODITIES | furs ltd |
| 20170180128 | METHOD FOR MANAGING A TRUSTED IDENTITY | GEMALTO, INC.; |
| 5908744 | Detecting Mycobacterium tuberculosis by nucleic acid sequence amplification | GEN-PROBE INCORPORATED; |
| 20170230791 | SYSTEMS, METHODS AND APPARATUS FOR GEOFENCE NETWORKS | GEOFRENZY, INC.; |
| 20170316162 | DISTRIBUTED SYSTEMS FOR SECURE STORAGE AND RETRIEVAL OF ENCRYPTED BIOLOGICAL SPECIMEN DATA | GLOBAL SPECIMEN SOLUTIONS, INC.; |
| 6061449 | Secure processor with external memory using block chaining and block re-ordering | GOOGLE TECHNOLOGY HOLDINGS LLC; |
| 20170201582 | CROSS-PROTOCOL DISTRIBUTED CLOUD STORAGE SYSTEM AND DATA MANAGEMENT METHOD BASED ON OPERATION CONTROL UNIT | GRADUATE SCHOOL AT SHENZHEN, TSINGHUA UNIVERSITY; |
| 20170195406 | DISTRIBUTED NETWORK NODE OPERATION SYSTEM BASED ON OPERATION CONTROL UNIT | GRADUATE SCHOOL AT SHENZHEN, TSINGHUA UNIVERSITY; |
| 20170126702 | VERIFICATION LINEAGE TRACKING AND TRANSFER CONTROL OF DATA SETS | GUARDTIME IP HOLDINGS LIMITED; |
| 20170295180 | System and Method for Access Control Using Context-Based Proof | GUARDTIME IP HOLDINGS LIMITED; |
| 20170041148 | BLOCKCHAIN-SUPPORTED DEVICE LOCATION VERIFICATION WITH DIGITAL SIGNATURES | GUARDTIME IP HOLDINGS LIMITED; |
| 9853819 | Blockchain-supported, node ID-augmented digital record signature method | GUARDTIME IP HOLDINGS LIMITED; |
| 20160267472 | SECURING DIGITAL GIFT CARDS WITH A PUBLIC LEDGER | GYFT |
| 20060005031 | Methods and systems for utilizing a single cryptographic integrity check to generate multiple cryptographic integrity check values for components of transcodable content | HEWLETT-PACKARD DEVELOPMENT COMPANY, L.P.; |
| 20050149739 | PIN verification using cipher block chaining | HEWLETT-PACKARD DEVELOPMENT COMPANY, L.P.; |
| 20080276041 | DATA STORAGE ARRAY SCALING METHOD AND SYSTEM WITH MINIMAL DATA MOVEMENT | HGST NETHERLANDS B.V.; |
| 8287749 | High-molecular thin film, pattern medium and manufacturing method thereof | HITACHI, LTD.; |
| 8039056 | Polymer thin film, patterned substrate, patterned medium for magnetic recording, and method of manufacturing these articles | HITACHI, LTD.; |
| 20170345011 | SYSTEM AND METHOD EXECUTED ON A BLOCKCHAIN NETWORK | Hitfin, Inc.; |

# US Blockchain Patents through February 2018

| Serial/Reg Number | Title | Patent Owner |
|---|---|---|
| 9872050 | Method for generating, providing and reproducing digital contents in conjunction with digital currency, and terminal and computer readable recording medium using same | HONG, JAY WU;UHR, JOON-SUN; |
| 20160261411 | METHOD AND SYSTEM OF PROVIDING AUTHENTICATION OF USER ACCESS TO A COMPUTER RESOURCE VIA A MOBILE DEVICE USING MULTIPLE SEPARATE SECURITY FACTORS | HOVERKEY |
| 20170019496 | NEEDS-MATCHING NAVIGATOR SYSTEM | OWNED BY INDIVIDUAL PERSON NOT CORPORATION |
| 20170353301 | Caravan | OWNED BY INDIVIDUAL PERSON NOT CORPORATION |
| 9849364 | Smart device | OWNED BY INDIVIDUAL PERSON NOT CORPORATION |
| 20170070778 | Personal Secure Event Recording Device | OWNED BY INDIVIDUAL PERSON NOT CORPORATION |
| 20160191243 | OUT-OF-BAND VALIDATION OF DOMAIN NAME SYSTEM RECORDS | OWNED BY INDIVIDUAL PERSON NOT CORPORATION |
| 9255419 | Cantilever parking lift | OWNED BY INDIVIDUAL PERSON NOT CORPORATION |
| 20120077085 | POSITIVE ELECTRODE FOR NON-AQUEOUS ELECTROLYTE BATTERYAND NON-AQUEOUS ELECTROLYTE BATTERY | OWNED BY INDIVIDUAL PERSON NOT CORPORATION |
| 7942086 | Hobble turning method and preferred applications for said method | OWNED BY INDIVIDUAL PERSON NOT CORPORATION |
| 4487396 | Scotch block attachment fitting | OWNED BY INDIVIDUAL PERSON NOT CORPORATION |
| 20170285720 | METHOD AND SYSTEM FOR MITIGATING TRANSMISSION CONGESTION VIA DISTRIBUTED COMPUTING AND BLOCKCHAIN TECHNOLOGY | OWNED BY INDIVIDUAL PERSON NOT CORPORATION |
| 20170262862 | METHOD AND APPARATUS FOR MANAGING AND PROVIDING PROVENANCE OF PRODUCT USING BLOCKCHAIN | OWNED BY INDIVIDUAL PERSON NOT CORPORATION |
| 20170206532 | SYSTEM AND METHOD FOR STREAMLINED REGISTRATION AND MANAGEMENT OF PRODUCTS OVER A COMMUNICATION NETWORK RELATED THERETO | OWNED BY INDIVIDUAL PERSON NOT CORPORATION |
| 9792101 | Capacity and automated de-install of linket mobile apps with deep links | OWNED BY INDIVIDUAL PERSON NOT CORPORATION |
| 20170052676 | VIRTUAL OBJECT REGISTRY AND TRACKING PLATFORM | OWNED BY INDIVIDUAL PERSON NOT CORPORATION |
| 20170031874 | Blockchain and deep links for mobile apps | OWNED BY INDIVIDUAL PERSON NOT CORPORATION |
| 9569771 | Method and system for storage and retrieval of blockchain blocks using galois fields | OWNED BY INDIVIDUAL PERSON NOT CORPORATION |
| 20160217436 | Method, System and Program Product for Tracking and Securing Transactions of Authenticated Items over Block Chain Systems. | OWNED BY INDIVIDUAL PERSON NOT CORPORATION |
| 20150348169 | SYSTEM AND METHOD FOR MARKETPLACE SOFTWARE PLATFORM | OWNED BY INDIVIDUAL PERSON NOT CORPORATION |
| 20170220998 | AUTOMATED SERVICE MANAGEMENT SYSTEM WITH RULE-BASED, CASCADING ACTION REQUESTS | OWNED BY INDIVIDUAL PERSON NOT CORPORATION |

# US Blockchain Patents through February 2018

| Serial/Reg Number | Title | Patent Owner |
|---|---|---|
| 20170221032 | System and method for machine learning based user application | OWNED BY INDIVIDUAL PERSON NOT CORPORATION |
| 20170048234 | Social Aggregating, Fractionally Efficient Transfer Guidance, Conditional Triggered Transaction, Datastructures, Apparatuses, Methods and Systems | OWNED BY INDIVIDUAL PERSON NOT CORPORATION |
| 20150379510 | Method and system to use a block chain infrastructure and Smart Contracts to monetize data transactions involving changes to data included into a data supply chain. | OWNED BY INDIVIDUAL PERSON NOT CORPORATION |
| 9313248 | Method and apparatus for delivering encoded content | OWNED BY INDIVIDUAL PERSON NOT CORPORATION |
| 20150348017 | METHOD FOR INTEGRATING CRYPTOCURRENCY TRANSFER ON A SOCIAL NETWORK INTERFACE | OWNED BY INDIVIDUAL PERSON NOT CORPORATION |
| 20160098723 | System and method for block-chain verification of goods | OWNED BY INDIVIDUAL PERSON NOT CORPORATION |
| 20170109955 | BLOCKCHAIN ELECTRONIC VOTING SYSTEM AND METHOD | OWNED BY INDIVIDUAL PERSON NOT CORPORATION |
| 20170061398 | CRYPTOGRAPHIC CURRENCY BLOCK CHAIN BASED VOTING SYSTEM | OWNED BY INDIVIDUAL PERSON NOT CORPORATION |
| 20170351660 | METHOD AND SYSTEM OF PROVISIONING ELECTRONIC FORMS | OWNED BY INDIVIDUAL PERSON NOT CORPORATION |
| 20170323392 | CONSENSUS SYSTEM FOR MANIPULATION RESISTANT DIGITAL RECORD KEEPING | OWNED BY INDIVIDUAL PERSON NOT CORPORATION |
| 20170286880 | System and method of a requirement, compliance and resource management | OWNED BY INDIVIDUAL PERSON NOT CORPORATION |
| 20170193464 | Protocol utilizing bitcoin blockchain for maintaining independently proposed and approved set contents | OWNED BY INDIVIDUAL PERSON NOT CORPORATION |
| 20170140375 | System and Method for Permissioned Distributed Block Chain | OWNED BY INDIVIDUAL PERSON NOT CORPORATION |
| 20170075941 | CONSENSUS SYSTEM AND METHOD FOR ADDING DATA TO A BLOCKCHAIN | OWNED BY INDIVIDUAL PERSON NOT CORPORATION |
| 20170243216 | DIGITAL PAYMENT PROCESSING UTILIZING ENCRYPTED COMPUTER NETWORKING | OWNED BY INDIVIDUAL PERSON NOT CORPORATION |
| 20170213287 | SYSTEM AND METHOD FOR PROVIDING A CRYPTOGRAPHIC PLATFORM FOR EXCHANGING DEBT SECURITIES DENOMINATED IN VIRTUAL CURRENCIES | OWNED BY INDIVIDUAL PERSON NOT CORPORATION |
| 20170213289 | Dividend Yielding Digital Currency through Elastic Securitization, High Frequency Cross Exchange Trading, and Smart Contracts | OWNED BY INDIVIDUAL PERSON NOT CORPORATION |
| 20150310476 | System and method for attention based currency | OWNED BY INDIVIDUAL PERSON NOT CORPORATION |
| 20150206106 | METHOD FOR CREATING, ISSUING AND REDEEMING PAYMENT ASSURED CONTRACTS BASED ON MATHEMEMATICALLY AND OBJECTIVELY VERIFIABLE CRITERIA | OWNED BY INDIVIDUAL PERSON NOT CORPORATION |
| 20170161991 | System and method for public verification of a gambling website or gaming event | OWNED BY INDIVIDUAL PERSON NOT CORPORATION |
| indiv | Board game apparatus and method | OWNED BY INDIVIDUAL PERSON NOT CORPORATION |

# US Blockchain Patents through February 2018

| Serial/Reg Number | Title | Patent Owner |
|---|---|---|
| 20170200147 | System and the computer methods of issuing, transferring and manipulating value or gift cards using blockchain technology | OWNED BY INDIVIDUAL PERSON NOT CORPORATION |
| 20170329996 | Authenticating Printed Paper Documents and Websites Against a Blockchain Record | OWNED BY INDIVIDUAL PERSON NOT CORPORATION |
| 20160212146 | PEDDaL Blockchaining for Document Integrity Verification Preparation | OWNED BY INDIVIDUAL PERSON NOT CORPORATION |
| 20160210444 | METHOD AND APPARATUS FOR DELIVERING ENCODED CONTENT | OWNED BY INDIVIDUAL PERSON NOT CORPORATION |
| 20150310497 | Method and process for registration, creation and management of micro shares of real or intangible properties and advertisements in a network system | OWNED BY INDIVIDUAL PERSON NOT CORPORATION |
| 20160117471 | MEDICAL EVENT LIFECYCLE MANAGEMENT | OWNED BY INDIVIDUAL PERSON NOT CORPORATION |
| 20160218879 | METHOD AND APPARATUS FOR THE LIMITATION OF THE MINING OF BLOCKS ON A BLOCK CHAIN | OWNED BY INDIVIDUAL PERSON NOT CORPORATION |
| 20180001184 | SMART DEVICE | OWNED BY INDIVIDUAL PERSON NOT CORPORATION |
| 20180012262 | COMPUTER IMPLEMENTED METHODS AND SYSTEM FOR TRADING KEYWORD(S) AND MANAGING REVENUE IN A SEARCH NETWORK | OWNED BY INDIVIDUAL PERSON NOT CORPORATION |
| 20180006990 | EXCLUSIVE SOCIAL NETWORK BASED ON CONSUMPTION OF LUXURY GOODS | OWNED BY INDIVIDUAL PERSON NOT CORPORATION |
| '20180034804' | "Portable Authentication and Encryption Device and System" | OWNED BY INDIVIDUAL PERSON NOT CORPORATION |
| '20180052462' | "MOBILE APPLICATION USER INTERFACE FOR EFFICIENTLY MANAGING AND ASSURING THE SAFETY, QUALITY AND SECURITY OF GOODS STORED WITHIN A TRUCK, TRACTOR OR TRAILER" | OWNED BY INDIVIDUAL PERSON NOT CORPORATION |
| '20180048485' | "INTEGRATED BUILDING MANAGEMENT SENSOR SYSTEM" | OWNED BY INDIVIDUAL PERSON NOT CORPORATION |
| 20170243179 | SYSTEM AND METHOD TO MONETIZE DIGITAL ARTWORK | OWNED BY INDIVIDUAL PERSON NOT CORPORATION |
| 20170270527 | ASSESSING TRUST TO FACILITATE BLOCKCHAIN TRANSACTIONS | OWNED BY INDIVIDUAL PERSON NOT CORPORATION |
| 20170359374 | Blockchain System with Nucleobase Sequencing as Proof of Work | INTEL CORPORATION; |
| 20170285633 | DRONE CONTROL REGISTRATION | INTEL CORPORATION; |
| 20170178072 | System, Apparatus And Method For Transferring Ownership Of A Smart Delivery Package | INTEL CORPORATION; |
| 20180006826 | PUBLIC KEY INFRASTRUCTURE USING BLOCKCHAINS | INTEL CORPORATION; |
| 20160364787 | SYSTEM, APPARATUS AND METHOD FOR MULTI-OWNER TRANSFER OF OWNERSHIP OF A DEVICE | INTEL CORPORATION; |
| 20170346848 | System, Apparatus And Method For Scalable Internet Of Things (IOT) Device On-Boarding With Quarantine Capabilities | INTEL CORPORATION; |
| 20180006807 | ENERGY-EFFICIENT BITCOIN MINING HARDWARE ACCELERATORS | INTEL CORPORATION; |
| 7200226 | Cipher block chaining decryption | INTEL CORPORATION; |
| 20170364908 | TECHNOLOGIES FOR DEVICE COMMISSIONING | INTEL CORPORATION; |
| 20160379212 | SYSTEM, APPARATUS AND METHOD FOR PERFORMING CRYPTOGRAPHIC OPERATIONS IN A TRUSTED EXECUTION ENVIRONMENT | INTEL CORPORATION; |

# US Blockchain Patents through February 2018

| Serial/Reg Number | Title | Patent Owner |
|---|---|---|
| 20170366347 | TECHNOLOGIES FOR DATA BROKER ASSISTED TRANSFER OF DEVICE OWNERSHIP | INTEL CORPORATION; |
| 20160284033 | ENERGY RESOURCE NETWORK | INTELLIGENT ENERGY LIMITED; |
| 20170212781 | PARALLEL EXECUTION OF BLOCKCHAIN TRANSACTIONS | INTERNATIONAL BUSINESS MACHINES CORPORATION; |
| 9858146 | Reducing latency for raid destage operations | INTERNATIONAL BUSINESS MACHINES CORPORATION; |
| 7908511 | File replacement in shared file system | INTERNATIONAL BUSINESS MACHINES CORPORATION; |
| 9824031 | Efficient clearinghouse transactions with trusted and un-trusted entities | INTERNATIONAL BUSINESS MACHINES CORPORATION; |
| 20170149819 | RESISTING REPLAY ATTACKS EFFICIENTLY IN A PERMISSIONED AND PRIVACY- PRESERVING BLOCKCHAIN NETWORK | INTERNATIONAL BUSINESS MACHINES CORPORATION; |
| 20170346907 | COORDINATING THE USE OF INDEPENDENT RADIO RECEIVERS ASSOCIATED WITH A SINGLE TRANSMITTER | INTERNATIONAL BUSINESS MACHINES CORPORATION; |
| 20170347253 | COORDINATING THE USE OF INDEPENDENT RADIO RECEIVERS ASSOCIATED WITH MULTIPLE DIFFERENT TRANSMITTERS | INTERNATIONAL BUSINESS MACHINES CORPORATION; |
| 20170213209 | ENTERPRISE BLOCKCHAINS AND TRANSACTIONAL SYSTEMS | INTERNATIONAL BUSINESS MACHINES CORPORATION; |
| 20170177898 | PERSONAL LEDGER BLOCKCHAIN | INTERNATIONAL BUSINESS MACHINES CORPORATION; |
| 8856479 | Implementing storage adapter performance optimization with hardware operations completion coalescence | INTERNATIONAL BUSINESS MACHINES CORPORATION; |
| 8544029 | Implementing storage adapter performance optimization with chained hardware operations minimizing hardware/firmware interactions | INTERNATIONAL BUSINESS MACHINES CORPORATION; |
| 4601012 | Zone partitioning in volume recovery system | INTERNATIONAL BUSINESS MACHINES CORPORATION; |
| 20170279774 | Decentralized Autonomous Edge Compute Coordinated by Smart Contract On A Blockchain | INTERNATIONAL BUSINESS MACHINES CORPORATION; |
| 20170140394 | CONSENSUS-BASED REPUTATION TRACKING IN ONLINE MARKETPLACES | INTERNATIONAL BUSINESS MACHINES CORPORATION; |
| '20180053161' | "TRACKING TRANSACTIONS THROUGH A BLOCKCHAIN" | INTERNATIONAL BUSINESS MACHINES CORPORATION; |
| 9513627 | Autonomous coordination of resources amongst robots | INVIA ROBOTICS, INC.;inVia Robotics, LLC; |
| 20160292396 | SYSTEM AND METHOD FOR AUTHENTICATING DIGITAL CONTENT | Iperial, Inc.; |
| 4807692 | Mold apparatus for endless track type continuous casting machine | Ishikawajima-Harima Jukogyo Kabushiki Kaisha;Nippon Kokan Kabushiki Kaisha; |
| '20180046992' | "SYSTEMS AND METHODS FOR ACCOUNT RECONCILIATION USING A DISTRIBUTED LEDGER" | JPMORGAN CHASE BANK, N.A.; |
| '20180047111' | "SYSTEMS AND METHODS FOR ENHANCED ORGANIZATIONAL TRANSPARENCY USING A CREDIT CHAIN" | JPMORGAN CHASE BANK, N.A.; |
| 20070166272 | HAIR COSMETIC COMPOSITIONS AND PROCESS FOR PRODUCING THE SAME | KAO CORPORATION; |
| 8003085 | Water-based shampoo | KAO CORPORATION; |
| 7964179 | Cosmetic hair preparation | KAO CORPORATION; |

# US Blockchain Patents through February 2018

| Serial/Reg Number | Title | Patent Owner |
|---|---|---|
| 20020060061 | Apparatus for manufacturing sheet metals through both sheet-casting process and continuous shear-straining process | KOREA INSTITUTE OF SCIENCE AND TECHNOLOGY; |
| 20160002826 | FIBER, FABRIC, AND NONWOVEN FABRIC | KURARAY CO., LTD.; |
| 9849197 | Switching-type fluorescent nanoparticle probe, and fluorescent molecular imaging method using same | KYOTO UNIVERSITY;SHIMADZU CORPORATION; |
| 9370589 | Switching fluorescent nanoparticle probe and fluorescent particle imaging method using same | KYOTO UNIVERSITY;SHIMADZU CORPORATION; |
| 20170214522 | SYSTEM AND PROCESS FOR TOKENIZATION OF DIGITAL MEDIA | loyall |
| 20170264428 | DATA STORAGE SYSTEM WITH BLOCKCHAIN TECHNOLOGY | MANIFOLD TECHNOLOGY, INC.; |
| 20170228371 | BLOCKCHAIN-ENHANCED DATABASE | MANIFOLD TECHNOLOGY, INC.; |
| 20170124556 | EVENT SYNCHRONIZATION SYSTEMS AND METHODS | MANIFOLD TECHNOLOGY, INC.; |
| 20160306982 | SYSTEM AND METHOD FOR PROVIDING A CRYPTOGRAPHIC PLATFORM FOR EXCHANGING INFORMATION | MANIFOLD TECHNOLOGY, INC.; |
| 9397985 | System and method for providing a cryptographic platform for exchanging information | MANIFOLD TECHNOLOGY, INC.; |
| 20180013567 | METHOD AND SYSTEM FOR VERIFICATION OF IDENTITY ATTRIBUTE INFORMATION | MASTERCARD INTERNATIONAL INCORPORATED; |
| 20170344580 | METHOD AND SYSTEM FOR TRANSFERRING TRUST ACROSS BLOCK CHAIN SEGMENTS | MASTERCARD INTERNATIONAL INCORPORATED; |
| 20170344435 | METHOD AND SYSTEM FOR DESYNCHRONIZATION RECOVERY FOR PERMISSIONED BLOCKCHAINS USING BLOOM FILTERS | MASTERCARD INTERNATIONAL INCORPORATED; |
| 20170346693 | METHOD AND SYSTEM FOR EFFICIENT DISTRIBUTION OF CONFIGURATION DATA UTILIZING PERMISSIONED BLOCKCHAIN TECHNOLOGY | MASTERCARD INTERNATIONAL INCORPORATED; |
| 20170323294 | METHOD AND SYSTEM FOR INSTANTANEOUS PAYMENT USING RECORDED GUARANTEES | MASTERCARD INTERNATIONAL INCORPORATED; |
| 20170148016 | METHOD AND SYSTEM FOR GROSS SETTLEMENT BY USE OF AN OPAQUE BLOCKCHAIN | MASTERCARD INTERNATIONAL INCORPORATED; |
| 20170132625 | METHOD AND SYSTEM FOR USE OF A BLOCKCHAIN IN A TRANSACTION PROCESSING NETWORK | MASTERCARD INTERNATIONAL INCORPORATED; |
| 20170132626 | METHOD AND SYSTEM FOR PROCESSING OF A BLOCKCHAIN TRANSACTION IN A TRANSACTION PROCESSING NETWORK | MASTERCARD INTERNATIONAL INCORPORATED; |
| 20160342976 | METHOD AND SYSTEM FOR LINKAGE OF BLOCKCHAIN-BASED ASSETS TO FIAT CURRENCY ACCOUNTS | MASTERCARD INTERNATIONAL INCORPORATED; |
| 9870562 | Method and system for integration of market exchange and issuer processing for blockchain-based transactions | MASTERCARD INTERNATIONAL INCORPORATED; |
| 20160342989 | METHOD AND SYSTEM FOR PROCESSING BLOCKCHAIN-BASED TRANSACTIONS ON EXISTING PAYMENT NETWORKS | MASTERCARD INTERNATIONAL INCORPORATED; |
| 20170134280 | METHOD AND SYSTEM FOR VALIDATION OF HASHED DATA VIA ACCEPTANCE FRAMES | MASTERCARD INTERNATIONAL INCORPORATED; |
| 20170352033 | METHOD AND SYSTEM FOR AUTHORIZATION USING A PUBLIC LEDGER AND ENCRYPTION KEYS | MASTERCARD INTERNATIONAL INCORPORATED; |
| 20170207917 | METHOD AND SYSTEM FOR DISTRIBUTED CRYPTOGRAPHIC KEY PROVISIONING AND STORAGE VIA ELLIPTIC CURVE CRYPTOGRAPHY | MASTERCARD INTERNATIONAL INCORPORATED; |

# US Blockchain Patents through February 2018

| Serial/Reg Number | Title | Patent Owner |
|---|---|---|
| 20170180134 | METHOD AND SYSTEM FOR BLOCKCHAIN VARIANT USING DIGITAL SIGNATURES | MASTERCARD INTERNATIONAL INCORPORATED; |
| 20160342994 | METHOD AND SYSTEM FOR FRAUD CONTROL OF BLOCKCHAIN-BASED TRANSACTIONS | MASTERCARD INTERNATIONAL INCORPORATED; |
| 20170357966 | METHOD AND SYSTEM FOR USE OF A PROPRIETARY PRIVATE BLOCKCHAIN | MASTERCARD INTERNATIONAL INCORPORATED; |
| 20170344987 | METHOD AND SYSTEM FOR AN EFFICIENT CONSENSUS MECHANISM FOR PERMSSIONED BLOCKCHAINS USING BLOOM FILTERS AND AUDIT GUARANTEES | MASTERCARD INTERNATIONAL INCORPORATED; |
| 20170236121 | METHOD AND SYSTEM FOR OFFLINE BLOCKCHAIN EXCHANGES | MASTERCARD INTERNATIONAL INCORPORATED; |
| 20170221022 | INFORMATION TRANSACTION INFRASTRUCTURE | MASTERCARD INTERNATIONAL INCORPORATED; |
| 20170169363 | Integrated System of Search, Commerce and Analytics Engines Supported by Beacons, Mobile Consumer and Merchant Applications Which Discover, Connect to, Report on, Communicate and Transact with Places, People and Objects Based on Their Proximal, Ephemeral and Analytical Attributes on a Symmetric Basis | Max2 Inc. |
| 20170091467 | PROVABLE TRACEABILITY | MCAFEE, LLC; |
| 20170353309 | CRYPTOGRAPHIC APPLICATIONS FOR A BLOCKCHAIN SYSTEM | MICROSOFT TECHNOLOGY LICENSING, LLC; |
| 8677336 | Block count based procedure layout and splitting | MICROSOFT TECHNOLOGY LICENSING, LLC; |
| 20170287593 | SYSTEMS FOR MULTIPLE LEGAL GAME PROVIDERS AND MULTIPLE JURISDICTIONS WITH BLOCK CHAIN | MIDO PLAY |
| 6716918 | Methacrylate-based polymer and process for producing the same | MITSUBISHI CHEMICAL CORPORATION; |
| 20160321676 | SHARING CONTENT WITHIN SOCIAL NETWORK SERVICES | MONEGRAPH |
| 20160321675 | AUTHENTICATING CONTENT AT AN ONLINE CONTENT MANAGEMENT SYSTEM | MONEGRAPH |
| 20160321769 | ONLINE CONTENT MANAGEMENT AND MARKETPLACE PLATFORM | MONEGRAPH |
| 20160323109 | RIGHTS TRANSFERS USING BLOCK CHAIN TRANSACTIONS | MONEGRAPH |
| 20160328713 | Identity Management Service Using A Blockchain Providing Identity Transactions Between Devices | MONEGRAPH |
| 20160321434 | DIGITAL CONTENT RIGHTS TRANSACTIONS USING BLOCK CHAIN SYSTEMS | MONEGRAPH |
| 20160321435 | MANAGING DIGITAL CONTENT VIA BLOCK CHAIN REGISTERS | MONEGRAPH |
| 20160321629 | DIGITAL CONTENT RIGHTS TRANSFERS WITHIN SOCIAL NETWORKS | MONEGRAPH |
| 20180012324 | COMMUNICATION FLOW FOR VERIFICATION AND IDENTIFICATION CHECK | Morpho Trust USA |
| 4274085 | Flexible mode DES system | MOTOROLA, INC.; |
| 20170286951 | Dynamic Delivery Authorization for Cryptographic Payments | MOVING MEDIA |
| 20170032365 | CRYPTO-CURRENCY-BASED ACCRUED VALUE INTEROPERABILITY | MOZIDO, INC.; |
| 20160359637 | Distributed Function Hybrid Integrated Array | MPOWER TECHNOLOGY, INC.; |
| 20150332283 | HEALTHCARE TRANSACTION VALIDATION VIA BLOCKCHAIN PROOF-OF-WORK, SYSTEMS AND METHODS | NANT HOLDINGS IP, LLC; |

# US Blockchain Patents through February 2018

| Serial/Reg Number | Title | Patent Owner |
|---|---|---|
| 20170005804 | SYSTEMS AND METHODS OF SECURE PROVENANCE FOR DISTRIBUTED TRANSACTION DATABASES | NASDAQ |
| 20180006831 | SYSTEMS AND METHODS FOR STORING AND SHARING TRANSACTIONAL DATA USING DISTRIBUTED COMPUTING SYSTEMS | NASDAQ |
| 9794074 | Systems and methods for storing and sharing transactional data using distributed computing systems | NASDAQ TECHNOLOGY AB; |
| 20170330174 | APPLICATION FRAMEWORK USING BLOCKCHAIN-BASED ASSET OWNERSHIP | NASDAQ, INC.; |
| 20170220815 | SYSTEMS AND METHODS FOR SECURING AND DISSEMINATING TIME SENSITIVE INFORMATION USING A BLOCKCHAIN | NASDAQ, INC.; |
| 20160292672 | SYSTEMS AND METHODS OF BLOCKCHAIN TRANSACTION RECORDATION | NASDAQ, INC.; |
| 9858569 | Systems and methods in support of authentication of an item | NAVARATNAM, RAMANAN; |
| 20170236094 | BLOCKCHAIN-BASED CROWDSOURCED INITIATIVES TRACKING SYSTEM | NETSPECTIVE COMMUNICATIONS LLC; |
| 20170149560 | DIGITAL BLOCKCHAIN AUTHENTICATION | NETSPECTIVE COMMUNICATIONS LLC; |
| 20170140145 | COMPUTER-CONTROLLED PHYSICALLY DISTRIBUTED COLLABORATIVE ASYNCHRONOUS DIGITAL TRANSACTIONS | NETSPECTIVE COMMUNICATIONS LLC; |
| 20170103167 | BLOCKCHAIN SYSTEM FOR NATURAL LANGUAGE PROCESSING | NETSPECTIVE COMMUNICATIONS LLC; |
| 9870591 | Distributed electronic document review in a blockchain system and computerized scoring based on textual and visual feedback | NETSPECTIVE COMMUNICATIONS LLC; |
| 20170091397 | DEVICE-DRIVEN NON-INTERMEDIATED BLOCKCHAIN SYSTEM OVER A SOCIAL INTEGRITY NETWORK | NETSPECTIVE COMMUNICATIONS LLC; |
| 9553982 | System and methods for tamper proof interaction recording and timestamping | NEWVOICEMEDIA LIMITED; |
| 9842216 | System and methods for tamper proof interaction recording and timestamping | NEWVOICEMEDIA, LTD.; |
| 20180012433 | VEHICLE IDENTIFICATION OR AUTHENTICATION | NIO USA |
| 9562128 | Copolymer | NIPPON SODA CO., LTD.; |
| 9018311 | Copolymer | NIPPON SODA CO., LTD.; |
| 9217052 | Copolymer | NIPPON SODA CO., LTD.; |
| 9115239 | Copolymer | NIPPON SODA CO., LTD.; |
| 8142929 | Positive electrode for non-aqueous electrolyte battery and non-aqueous electrolyte battery | NIPPON SODA CO., LTD.; |
| 7968229 | Positive electrode for non-aqueous electrolyte battery and non-aqueous electrolyte battery | NIPPON SODA CO., LTD.; |
| 7645830 | Polymer, crosslinked polymer, composition for solid polymer electrolyte, solid polymer electrolyte, and adhesive composition | NIPPON SODA CO., LTD.; |
| 7678860 | Composition for polymer solid electrolyte, polymer solid electrolyte, polymer, polymer solid electrolyte battery, ionconductive membrane, copolymer and process for producing the copolymer | NIPPON SODA CO., LTD.; |
| 7579401 | Solid polymer electrolyte | NIPPON SODA CO., LTD.; |
| 20160342977 | DEVICE, METHOD AND SYSTEM FOR VIRTUAL ASSET TRANSACTIONS | NUMERIC JUICE PTY LTD; |
| 20170091726 | LOW BANDWIDTH CRYPTO CURRENCY TRANSACTION EXECUTION AND SYNCHRONIZATION METHOD AND SYSTEM | NXT-ID, INC.; |
| 20170053249 | Electronic Crypto-Currency Management Method and System | NXT-ID, INC.; |
| 8744076 | Method and apparatus for encrypting data to facilitate resource savings and tamper detection | ORACLE INTERNATIONAL CORPORATION; |
| 20170115976 | MANAGING HIGHLY SCALABLE CONTINUOUS DELIVERY PIPELINES | ORACLE INTERNATIONAL CORPORATION; |

# US Blockchain Patents through February 2018

| Serial/Reg Number | Title | Patent Owner |
|---|---|---|
| 20170011460 | SYSTEMS AND METHODS FOR TRADING, CLEARING AND SETTLING SECURITIES TRANSACTIONS USING BLOCKCHAIN TECHNOLOGY | OUISA, LLC; |
| 20110170687 | CONTENT DECODING APPARATUS, CONTENT DECODING METHOD AND INTEGRATED CIRCUIT | PANASONIC CORPORATION; |
| 8058896 | Flexible parallel/serial reconfigurable array configuration scheme | PANASONIC CORPORATION; |
| 20170109636 | Crowd-Based Model for Identifying Executions of a Business Process | PANAYA LTD.; |
| 20170109637 | Crowd-Based Model for Identifying Nonconsecutive Executions of a Business Process | PANAYA LTD.; |
| 20170109670 | Crowd-Based Patterns for Identifying Executions of Business Processes | PANAYA LTD.; |
| 20170109638 | Ensemble-Based Identification of Executions of a Business Process | PANAYA LTD.; |
| 20170109667 | Automaton-Based Identification of Executions of a Business Process | PANAYA LTD.; |
| 20170109639 | General Model for Linking Between Nonconsecutively Performed Steps in Business Processes | PANAYA LTD.; |
| 20170109640 | Generation of Candidate Sequences Using Crowd-Based Seeds of Commonly-Performed Steps of a Business Process | PANAYA LTD.; |
| 20170109668 | Model for Linking Between Nonconsecutively Performed Steps in a Business Process | PANAYA LTD.; |
| '20180048461' | "APPARATUS, SYSTEM, AND METHODS FOR A BLOCKCHAIN IDENTITY TRANSLATOR" | PEER LEDGER INC |
| 20160365978 | MAKING CRYPTOGRAPHIC CLAIMS ABOUT STORED DATA USING AN ANCHORING SYSTEM | PEERNOVA |
| 20160283920 | AUTHENTICATION AND VERIFICATION OF DIGITAL DATA UTILIZING BLOCKCHAIN TECHNOLOGY | PEERNOVA |
| 20160358161 | SYSTEMS AND METHODS FOR AN ONLINE MUSIC MARKETPLACE | PEERTRACKS INC.; |
| 20170297389 | CHAIN FOR MOUNTING ON A VEHICLE TIRE | PEWAG SCHNEEKETTEN GMBH; |
| 20170243239 | Incentivized navigation | PIEXELBERG HOLDING GROUP |
| 6157964 | Method for specifying concurrent execution of a string of I/O command blocks in a chain structure | PMC-SIERRA, INC.; |
| 5923896 | Method for sequencing execution of I/O command blocks in a chain structure by setting hold-off flags and configuring a counter in each I/O command block | PMC-SIERRA, INC.; |
| 5892969 | Method for concurrently executing a configured string of concurrent I/O command blocks within a chain to perform a raid 5 I/O operation | PMC-SIERRA, INC.; |
| 5850567 | Method for specifying concurrent execution of a string of I/O command blocks in a chain structure | PMC-SIERRA, INC.; |
| 5812877 | I/O command block chain structure in a memory | PMC-SIERRA, INC.; |
| 5797034 | Method for specifying execution of only one of a pair of I/O command blocks in a chain structure | PMC-SIERRA, INC.; |
| 5768621 | Chain manager for use in executing a chain of I/O command blocks | PMC-SIERRA, INC.; |
| 5758187 | Method for enhancing performance of a RAID 1 read operation using a pair of I/O command blocks in a chain structure | PMC-SIERRA, INC.; |
| 20170372300 | SYSTEM AND METHOD FOR CRYPTOGRAPHICALLY VERIFIED DATA DRIVEN CONTRACTS | POKITDOK, INC.; |
| 20170039330 | SYSTEM AND METHOD FOR DECENTRALIZED AUTONOMOUS HEALTHCARE ECONOMY PLATFORM | POKITDOK, INC.; |
| 7744919 | Block copolymer micelle composition having an enhanced drug-loading capacity and sustained release | POSTECH FOUNDATION; |
| 20170373859 | Cryptographic Signature System and Related Systems and Methods | Praxik LLC |

# US Blockchain Patents through February 2018

| Serial/Reg Number | Title | Patent Owner |
|---|---|---|
| 20170300876 | CRYPTOCONOMY SOLUTION FOR ADMINISTRATION AND GOVERNANCE IN A DISTRIBUTED SYSTEM | PRICEWATERHOUSECOOPERS LLP; |
| 20180013707 | METHOD AND SYSTEM FOR SENDER-CONTROLLED MESSAGING AND CONTENT SHARING | PRIVATE GIANT |
| 20170338963 | DECENTRALIZED EXCHANGES IN A DISTRIBUTED AUTONOMOUS PLATFORM | PROTOBLOCK, INC.; |
| '20180034636' | "METHOD AND SYSTEM FOR CREATING PUBLIC RANDOMNESS" | QED-it Systems LTD; |
| '20180048463' | "METHOD AND SYSTEM FOR GENERATING PRIVATE RANDOMNESS FOR THE CREATION OF PUBLIC RANDOMNESS" | QED-it Systems LTD; |
| 20160283939 | SYSTEM AND METHOD TO PREVENT LOSS OF BITCOINS DUE TO ADDRESS ERRORS | QUALCOMM INCORPORATED; |
| 20170352012 | SECURE PROCESSING OF ELECTRONIC TRANSACTIONS BY A DECENTRALIZED, DISTRIBUTED LEDGER SYSTEM | R3 LTD.; |
| 20170372391 | DETERMINING EXCHANGE ITEM COMPLIANCE IN AN EXCHANGE ITEM MARKETPLACE NETWORK | Raise Marketplace Inc.; |
| 9167714 | Reverse wedgelock device | RAYTHEON COMPANY; |
| '20180048738' | "BLOCKCHAIN MANAGEMENT USING A DEVICE IN A WIRELESS TELECOMMUNICATION SYSTEM" | RED HAT, INC.; |
| 20160275461 | AUTOMATED ATTESTATION OF DEVICE INTEGRITY USING THE BLOCK CHAIN | RIVETZ CORP.; |
| 9758670 | Polycarbonate composition | SABIC GLOBAL TECHNOLOGIES B.V.; |
| 9169391 | Polycarbonate composition | SABIC GLOBAL TECHNOLOGIES B.V.; |
| 9169395 | Polycarbonate composition and articles formed therefrom | SABIC GLOBAL TECHNOLOGIES B.V.; |
| 20170359288 | MESSAGING SYSTEMS AND METHODS THAT EMPLOY A BLOCKCHAIN TO ENSURE INTEGRITY OF MESSAGE DELIVERY | SALESFORCE.COM, INC.; |
| 9806072 | Super CMOS devices on a microelectronics system | SCHOTTKY LSI, INC.; |
| 20160321278 | METHOD AND SYSTEM FOR ADDRESSING THE PROBLEM OF DISCOVERING RELEVANT SERVICES AND APPLICATIONS THAT ARE AVAILABLE OVER THE INTERNET OR OTHER COMMUNCATIONS NETWORK | SENSORIANT, INC.; |
| 20170301031 | CONFIRMATION AND RATING OF USER GENERATED ACTIVITIES | SENSORIANT, INC.; |
| 20170195336 | Method and System for Non-Authoritative Identity and Identity Permissions Broker and Use Thereof | SENSORMATIC ELECTRONICS, LLC; |
| 20170154331 | SYSTEMS AND METHODS FOR IMPROVING SECURITY IN BLOCKCHAIN-ASSET EXCHANGE | SHAPESHIFT AG; |
| 5512336 | Liquid crystal display device | SHARP KABUSHIKI KAISHA; |
| 20170151335 | SKIN EXTERNAL PREPARATION AND SKIN IRRITATION-REDUCING METHOD | SHIMADZU CORPORATION; |
| 20110104056 | NOVEL MOLECULAR ASSEMBLY, MOLECULAR PROBE FOR MOLECULAR IMAGING AND MOLECULAR PROBE FOR DRUG DELIVERY SYSTEM USING THE SAME, AND MOLECULAR IMAGING SYSTEM AND DRUG DELIVERY SYSTEM | SHIMADZU CORPORATION; |
| 6322924 | Preparation of crosslinked solid polymer electrolyte | SHIN-ETSU CHEMICAL CO., LTD.; |
| 6096234 | Cross-linked polymer solid electrolyte, method of manufacturing cross-linked solid polymer electrolyte, composite solid electrolyte, and thin solid cell employing composite solid electrolyte | SHIN-ETSU CHEMICAL CO., LTD.; |
| 6025437 | Block-graft copolymer, self-crosslinked polymer solid electrolyte and composite solid electrolyte manufactured through use of the block-graft copolymer, and solid cell employing the composite solid electrolyte | SHIN-ETSU CHEMICAL CO., LTD.; |

# US Blockchain Patents through February 2018

| Serial/Reg Number | Title | Patent Owner |
|---|---|---|
| 20170302450 | Identity Management Service Using A Blockchain Providing Certifying Transactions Between Devices | shocard |
| 9722790 | Identity management service using a blockchain providing certifying transactions between devices | SHOCARD, INC.; |
| 20160330035 | User Identification Management System and Method | SHOCARD, INC.; |
| 20170257358 | Method and System for Authenticated Login Using Static or Dynamic Codes | SHOCARD, INC.; |
| 20170358168 | SYSTEMS AND METHODS FOR WIRELESS CHARGING STATIONS | SICHUAN ENERGY INTERNET RESEARCH INSTITUTE, TSINGHUA UNIVERSITY; |
| 4244460 | Process and equipment to form modules of biscuits or other like products | Siemens |
| 20160379330 | METHOD AND APPARATUS FOR PROTECTING DIGITAL PHOTOS FROM ALTERATION | SIGNS & WONDERS UNLIMITED, LLC; |
| 20170243193 | HYBRID BLOCKCHAIN | SKUCHAIN, INC.; |
| 20160164884 | CRYPTOGRAPHIC VERIFICATION OF PROVENANCE IN A SUPPLY CHAIN | SKUCHAIN, INC.; |
| 20170237553 | METHOD AND APPARATUS FOR PROVIDING A UNIVERSAL DETERMINISTICALLY REPRODUCIBLE CRYPTOGRAPHIC KEY-PAIR REPRESENTATION FOR ALL SKUs, SHIPPING CARTONS, AND ITEMS | SKUCHAIN, INC.; |
| 9641338 | Method and apparatus for providing a universal deterministically reproducible cryptographic key-pair representation for all SKUs, shipping cartons, and items | SKUCHAIN, INC.; |
| 9641342 | Tracking unitization occurring in a supply chain | SKUCHAIN, INC.; |
| 9436923 | Tracking unitization occurring in a supply chain | SKUCHAIN, INC.; |
| 6964049 | Smart internetworking operating system for low computational power microprocessors | Smartmatic Corporation; |
| 20170111385 | RISK ASSESSMENT USING SOCIAL NETWORKING DATA | SOCURE INC.; |
| 9558524 | Risk assessment using social networking data | SOCURE INC.; |
| 4653595 | Method and apparatus for remote release of hammer and follow block chain connection | SOLOCO, INC..; |
| 20170310653 | CLIENT, SERVER, METHOD AND IDENTITY VERIFICATION SYSTEM | SONY CORPORATION; |
| 20170346833 | BLOCKCHAIN-BASED SYSTEM, AND ELECTRONIC APPARATUS AND METHOD IN THE SYSTEM | SONY CORPORATION; |
| 20170346637 | ELECTRONIC APPARATUS, METHOD FOR ELECTRONIC APPARATUS AND INFORMATION PROCESSING SYSTEM | SONY CORPORATION; |
| 20170300877 | SYSTEM AND METHOD FOR PROVIDING SHARED HASH ENGINES ARCHITECTURE FOR A BITCOIN BLOCK CHAIN | Spondoolies Tech |
| 9830593 | Cryptographic currency user directory data and enhanced peer-verification ledger synthesis through multi-modal cryptographic key-address mapping | SS8 NETWORKS, INC.; |
| 20170250815 | SYSTEMS AND METHODS FOR CERTIFICATION OF DATA UNITS AND/OR CERTIFICATION VERIFICATION | STAMPERY INC.; |
| 9679276 | Systems and methods for using a block chain to certify the existence, integrity, and/or ownership of a file or communication | STAMPERY, INC. |
| 20170308920 | POINT MANAGEMENT APPARATUS, SYSTEM, AND METHOD | STOCK POINT INC.; |
| 20160379312 | MACHINE/ARTICLE/COMPOSITION/PROCESS STATE(S) FOR TRACKING PHILANTHROPIC AND/OR OTHER EFFORTS | SUNLIGHT PAYMENTS, INC.; |
| 20170243176 | Block Mining Methods and Apparatus | Sunrise Tech Group, LLC |
| 20170132620 | SYSTEMS AND METHODS FOR AUTONOMOUS DEVICE TRANSACTING | SWFL, Inc., d/b/a "Filament",RENO,NV,US SWF MACHINERY INC,"SWF Machinery, Inc.; |

# US Blockchain Patents through February 2018

| Serial/Reg Number | Title | Patent Owner |
|---|---|---|
| 20170132621 | SYSTEMS AND METHODS FOR AUTONOMOUS DEVICE TRANSACTING | SWFL, Inc., d/b/a "Filament",RENO,NV,US SWG SCHRAUBENWEK GAISBACH GMBH,SWG Schraubenwek Gaisbach GmbH,WALDENBURG,,DE SWG SCHRAUBENWERK GAISBACH GMBH & CO,SWG SCHRAUBENWERK GAISBACH GMBH (1/2 INTEREST),WALDENBURG,, DE S & W HLDGS INC,"S&W HOLDING, INC.; |
| 7705753 | Methods, systems and computer-readable media for compressing data | SYTEX, INC.; |
| 20170295021 | METHOD TO ASSURE CORRECT DATA PACKET TRAVERSAL THROUGH A PARTICULAR PATH OF A NETWORK | TELEFONICA, S.A.; |
| 20170357009 | ON-BOARD BACKUP AND ANTI-SPOOFING GPS SYSTEM | THE BOEING COMPANY; |
| 20170192994 | SYSTEMS AND METHODS CONCERNING TRACKING MODELS FOR DIGITAL INTERACTIONS | THE GRÄT NETWORK, PBC; |
| 20170324711 | Method for establishing, securing and transferring computer readable information using peer-to-peer public and private key cryptography | THE REAL MCCOY, LLC INC.; |
| 20170287068 | SYSTEMS AND METHODS FOR PROVIDING FINANCIAL DATA TO FINANCIAL INSTRUMENTS IN A DISTRIBUTED LEDGER SYSTEM | THOMSON REUTERS GLOBAL RESOURCES UNLIMITED COMPANY; |
| 20170353311 | SYSTEMS AND METHODS FOR PROVIDING IDENTITY SCORES | THOMSON REUTERS GLOBAL RESOURCES;THOMSON REUTERS GLOBAL RESOURCES UNLIMITED COMPANY; |
| 20170177855 | METHODS AND SYSTEMS FOR IDENTITY CREATION, VERIFICATION AND MANAGEMENT | THOMSON REUTERS GLOBAL RESOURCES;THOMSON REUTERS GLOBAL RESOURCES UNLIMITED COMPANY;THOMSON REUTERS SPECIAL SERVICES LLC;TR ORGANISATION LIMITED; |
| 7735623 | Linearly actuated rotating handrail system for escalators and moving walkways | THYSSENKRUPP ELEVATOR (ES/PBB) LTD.;THYSSENKRUPP ELEVATOR INNOVATION CENTER, S.A.; |
| 20170318008 | ARTIFICIAL INTELLIGENCE ENCRYPTION MODEL (AIEM) WITH DEVICE AUTHORIZATION AND ATTACK DETECTION (DAAAD) | TITANIUM CRYPT, INC.; |
| 9696625 | Method of forming resist pattern | TOKYO OHKA KOGYO CO., LTD.; |
| 20170046664 | SYSTEMS AND METHODS FOR TRACKING AND TRANSFERRING OWNERSHIP OF CONNECTED DEVICES USING BLOCKCHAIN LEDGERS | TORONTO-DOMINION BANK, THE; |
| 20170046693 | SYSTEMS AND METHODS FOR DETECTING AND RESOLVING DATA INCONSISTENCIES AMONG NETWORKED DEVICES USING HYBRID PRIVATE-PUBLIC BLOCKCHAIN LEDGERS | TORONTO-DOMINION BANK, THE; |
| 20170046651 | SYSTEMS AND METHOD FOR TRACKING ENTERPRISE EVENTS USING HYBRID PUBLIC-PRIVATE BLOCKCHAIN LEDGERS | TORONTO-DOMINION BANK, THE; |

# US Blockchain Patents through February 2018

| Serial/Reg Number | Title | Patent Owner |
|---|---|---|
| 20170046652 | SYSTEMS AND METHOD FOR TRACKING BEHAVIOR OF NETWORKED DEVICES USING HYBRID PUBLIC-PRIVATE BLOCKCHAIN LEDGERS | TORONTO-DOMINION BANK, THE; |
| 20170046698 | SYSTEMS AND METHODS FOR ESTABLISHING AND ENFORCING TRANSACTION-BASED RESTRICTIONS USING HYBRID PUBLIC-PRIVATE BLOCKCHAIN LEDGERS | TORONTO-DOMINION BANK, THE; |
| 20170046792 | SYSTEMS AND METHOD FOR TRACKING SUBDIVIDED OWNERSHIP OF CONNECTED DEVICES USING BLOCK-CHAIN LEDGERS | TORONTO-DOMINION BANK, THE; |
| 20170046709 | PRODUCT TRACKING AND CONTROL SYSTEM | TORONTO-DOMINION BANK, THE; |
| 20170046526 | System and Method for Implementing Hybrid Public-Private Block-Chain Ledgers | TORONTO-DOMINION BANK, THE;TD Bank Group; |
| 9371427 | Pattern forming method | TOSHIBA MEMORY CORPORATION; |
| 9152053 | Method of forming pattern | TOSHIBA MEMORY CORPORATION; |
| 8808973 | Method of forming pattern | TOSHIBA MEMORY CORPORATION; |
| 8703407 | Pattern formation method | TOSHIBA MEMORY CORPORATION; |
| 8828747 | Pattern forming methods and semiconductor device manufacturing method | TOSHIBA MEMORY CORPORATION; |
| 8986488 | Pattern formation method and polymer alloy base material | TOSHIBA MEMORY CORPORATION; |
| 20170103468 | Use of Blockchain Based Distributed Consensus Control | TRANSACTIVE GRID INC.; |
| 7702104 | System and method for securing genomic information | TWITTER, INC.; |
| 20170344988 | SYSTEM AND METHOD FOR FACILITATING BLOCKCHAIN-BASED VALIDATION | UBS BUSINESS SOLUTIONS AG; |
| 9862222 | Digitally encoded seal for document verification | UIPCO, LLC; |
| 9855785 | Digitally encoded seal for document verification | UIPCO, LLC; |
| 5627840 | Memory based interface | UNISYS CORPORATION; |
| 9514293 | Behavioral profiling method and system to authenticate a user | United Services Automobile Association;UNITED SERVICES AUTOMOBILE ASSOCIATION (USAA); |
| 20170258714 | NANOVECTORS FOR PENETRATING BRAIN TUMOR TISSUES TO CONDUCT GENE THERAPY | UNIVERSITY OF HOUSTON SYSTEM; |
| 9870508 | Securely authenticating a recording file from initial collection through post-production and distribution | Unveiled Labs, Inc. |
| 20170286717 | METHOD AND SYSTEM FOR MANAGING PERSONAL INFORMATION WITHIN INDEPENDENT COMPUTER SYSTEMS AND DIGITAL NETWORKS | VCHAIN TECHNOLOGY LIMITED; |
| 20170116693 | Systems and Methods for Decentralizing Commerce and Rights Management for Digital Assets Using a Blockchain Rights Ledger | VERIMATRIX, INC.; |
| 20170237554 | METHODS AND SYSTEMS FOR USING DIGITAL SIGNATURES TO CREATE TRUSTED DIGITAL ASSET TRANSFERS | VISA INTERNATIONAL SERVICE ASSOCIATION; |
| 20160224977 | TOKEN CHECK OFFLINE | VISA INTERNATIONAL SERVICE ASSOCIATION; |
| 20170372417 | DIGITAL ASSET ACCOUNT MANAGEMENT | VISA INTERNATIONAL SERVICE ASSOCIATION; |
| 20170329980 | SECURE AND SCALABLE DATA TRANSFER USING A HYBRID BLOCKCHAIN-BASED APPROACH | VMWARE, INC.; |
| 20170147975 | UNMANNED AERIAL DELIVERY TO SECURE LOCATION | WALMART |
| 20170132393 | PRESCRIPTION HOME DELIVERY | WALMART |
| 20170013047 | SYSTEMS AND METHODS FOR ELECTRONIC DATA DISTRIBUTION | WHETHER OR KNOT LLC |
| 9807067 | Decentralized authoritative messaging | WICKR INC.; |
| 9673973 | Decentralized authoritative messaging | WICKR INC.; |
| 9590956 | Decentralized authoritative messaging | WICKR INC.; |

# US Blockchain Patents through February 2018

| Serial/Reg Number | Title | Patent Owner |
|---|---|---|
| '9892460' | "Systems, methods, and program products for operating exchange traded products holding digital math-based assets" | WINKLEVOSS IP, LLC; |
| '9898782' | "Systems, methods, and program products for operating exchange traded products holding digital math-based assets" | WINKLEVOSS IP, LLC; |
| 5608178 | Method of storing and editing performance data in an automatic performance device | YAMAHA CORPORATION; |
| 20150225176 | Zero tension system conveyor | ZERO TENSION SYSTEM, LLC; |
| 9010528 | Zero tension system conveyor | ZERO TENSION SYSTEM, LLC; |

# ABOUT THE AUTHOR

 Jennifer Wolfe is CEO of Dot Brand 360, a digital agency, and the principal of Wolfe Board Advisors, where she offers education and consulting for boards and C-suite executives on digital, data privacy and cybersecurity strategy, the impact of emerging technologies, management and compliance. She has also served as managing partner of the patent law firm Wolfe, Sadler, Breen, Morasch & Colby and was the first female president of the Greater Cincinnati Venture Capital Association. Her highly acclaimed books — *Digital in the Boardroom* (2016), *Domain Names Rewired* (2013) and *Brand Rewired* (2010) — have been endorsed by senior executives from Microsoft, Uber, Procter & Gamble, DC Entertainment, General Electric, Richemont, and the Motion Picture Association of America. She has written a regular column in *Click Z* and *Search Engine Watch* about future digital trends and was named one of the top IP strategists in the world by *IAM* magazine. She served on the GNSO Council of ICANN and subsequently chaired the Independent Review of the GNSO. She has a black belt in Six Sigma process improvement, is nationally accredited in public relations, a National Association of Corporate Directors Governance Fellow and certified in cybersecurity oversight by Carnegie Mellon's Software Engineering Institute. Jen is an alumna of the Direct Women Institute and completed the Stanford Law School Rock Center for Corporate Governance Program.

For more information, go to www.consultwolfe.com.

# DIGITAL ADVISOR
# KEYNOTER, HOST, MODERATOR

If you are interested in an executive briefing or mapping session to understand how blockchain could impact your industry and company, email Jen at jwolfe@consultwolfe.com.

Jen is also available to speak or provide educational briefings and assessments for your board or c-suite executives on a range of topics:

- ❖ Blockchain
- ❖ Digital Disruption
- ❖ Artificial Intelligence & IOT
- ❖ Data Privacy
- ❖ Global Internet Policy & Regulations
- ❖ Effective Collaboration Across Functions for Digital & Cybersecurity Initiatives
- ❖ Open Source Policy Best Practices
- ❖ Patent Analytics for Trend Forecasting
- ❖ General Counsel Best Practices in Cybersecurity Oversight

For more information, go to www.consultwolfe.com.

96929818R00074

Made in the USA
Columbia, SC
09 June 2018